How to Make
The Rest of Your Life

THE BEST
of YOUR LIFE

Victoria Rose

Testimonials for Victoria Rose

"Inspiring, positive, effective, energetic, fun and unforgettable."
– Christine Handley, Senior Lecturer

*"Enlightening and informative not only on
a professional level but also on a personal one."*
– Rozanne Patane, School Administrative Manager

"Engaging, motivating, knowledgeable and down to earth."
– Heather Strecker, Organisational Capability Support Officer

*"Victoria – dynamic, insightful, you make language such
a positive tool, so refreshing and challenging. Thank you."*
– Michelle Morales, Director, Early Childcare

*"A number of new ideas and revisited some old concepts
with a fresh approach."*
– Anne Dureau–Power, Administration Officer

"Lively, engaging, interesting and fun."
– Marie Nelson, Senior Manager, Human Resources for Health

"Rich in information, presented clearly, inspiring and fun."
– Sharon Konrabt, Director

From NOW To WOW

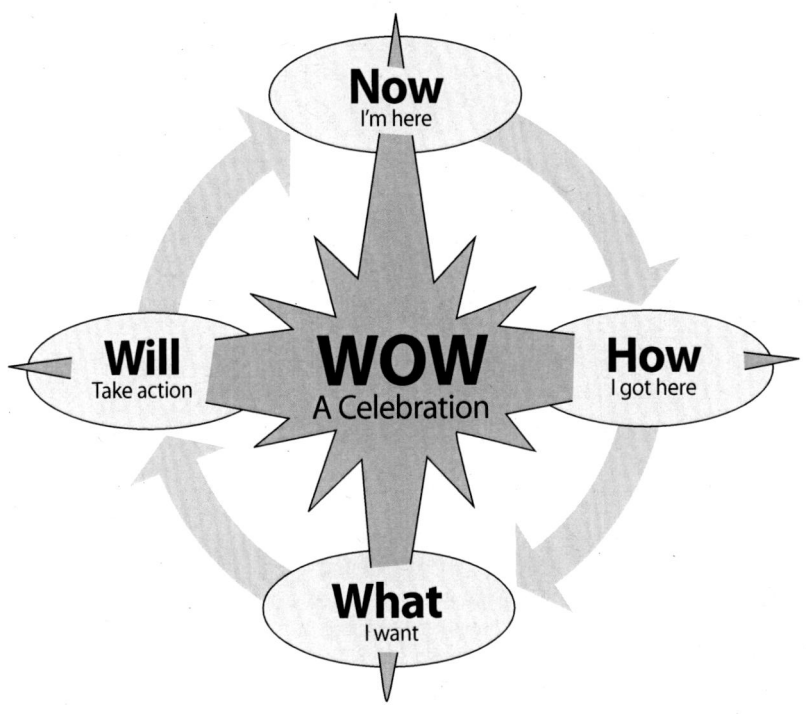

Be Courageous Be Confident Be You

How To Make The Rest Of Your Life The Best Of Your Life
First published in Australia in 2014 by Victoria Rose
PO Box 266
Port Melbourne Victoria 3207

Visit our website at:
www.Training2live.com.au
www.Over60StillFabulous.com

National Library of Australia Cataloguing-in-publications entry

Creator: Rose, Victoria
Title: How To Make The Rest Of Your Life The Best Of Your Life:
Tough Love For Smart Single Women Over 60

ISBN: 9780992579203 (paperback)

Subjects:
Personal Development
Self-actualization (Psychology) in women.
Women—Conduct of life
Adjustment (Psychology)

Dewey Number: 158.1

Editor: Paul Lonergan, Cavalletti Communications
(cavalletticommunications.com)
Proof Reader: Lindy Ferris
Cover and internal design: Pipeline Design
(pipelinedesign.com.au)
Author photo: Zedphotography
Makeup: Arbonne International ID 613271377
Printed in Australia by ExciteBooks 54505

Table of Contents

Introduction

Are you a smart, single woman over 60 who still feels fabulous? Or do you feel absolutely well past your use-by-date? Are you a quitter, or do you think you deserve to live a life full of energy, inspiration and fulfillment?

It's never too late to smell the roses

This book is a celebration of smart, single women over 60 and the many roles they play over their lifetime. But wait, by what criteria can you be deemed smart?

That's easy ... *you* deem yourself as smart, no outside authority is needed, is it?

For many baby boomers, outside authority *is* needed. Someone else's approval *is* necessary. That's a major reason for writing this book. I think we're grown up now; I believe we can grant approval to ourselves, to choose how to live our lives, can't we?

How did we get here?

People often make harsh statements about older people, but if we are past our use-by-date, who sets that date; who pulls those strings?

It turns out that control starts at the very beginning: a baby girl is born into a pink world with the road map of her life's journey already in place. This road map has been determined by her parents and by society and if she doesn't follow the route marked within she may pay a high and sometimes extremely harsh price. Isn't it time we broke free?

After a long life of habitual behaviour and ingrained responses, can women over 60 make those necessary changes? Absolutely they can! But only if they want to, only if *they* believe they can.

> # My mission: to shine the light on how women can liberate the power they possess.

Do not leave your future in someone else's hands. Embrace the possibilities of life.

The right to choose your own path is a sacred privilege. Use it. Sadly, few do.

How to Make The Rest of Your Life The Best of Your Life gives smart, single women over 60 a road map to a destination of their choosing. If you're sick of living on the Island of Lack, lack of courage, lack of confidence and lack of fun, then this book is for you. Working through a five-part formula in 'From NOW to WOW', you'll discover many signposts guiding you to living a happier life. As a confident and courageous woman, you too will stand up and say "I'm over 60 and I'm still fabulous!"

"Your life is an unwritten book that only you can write"
– Nietzsche

All case studies and stories used in this book are true and actual events. Only the names have been changed to protect the innocent and the guilty.

Why I Wrote This Book

Thirty-one years ago, as a soldier in the Australian Army Reserve, I discovered my ability to stand up and speak. In the following 23 years, I trained over 7,000 soldiers and officers in weapons, drill and theory and was promoted to the rank of Warrant Officer.

In 2008 I founded Training2live, a corporate training business providing 'Leadership with Integrity' workshops. I've travelled

"Let others lead small lives.
But not you.

Let others argue over small things.
But not you.

Let others cry over small hurts.
But not you.

Let others leave their future in
someone else's hands.
But not you."

-Jim Rohn

www.Over60StillFabulous.com

around Australia and NZ presenting workshops to over 12,500 participants from a diverse industry base. These included Rio Tinto, ANZ Bank, Australian Federal Police, Exmouth Hospital, Gold Coast Council, and the Australian Tax Department. Also Aged Care, Queensland Health, Fosterville Gold Mine, Swinburne University and The Ford Motor Company.

Now I have to confess, I think this is a pretty good effort for someone who not only stutters, but is also an introvert.

How cruel can our school years be?

That saying "Sticks and stones may break my bones but names will never hurt me" is a lie. The pain of falling off a branch with a stick in my mouth has long faded. The pain of cruel school taunts, such as 'porky pig' has also faded, but those words still sting.

Stuttering causes a baptism of fire

Regardless of my stutter, within months of joining the Army Reserve, Sergeant Blue marched me onto the parade ground to instruct a squad of ten soldiers in a basic drill lesson. Those first drill lessons were a humiliating failure, but they quickly caused me to discover how to manage my stutter. Yes I still stutter, but it's not the distressing problem it once was.

Introversion isn't easy either

As for being an introvert, my workshop participants rarely pick that. Most are adamant I am an extrovert. And that's the difference when you are passionate about what you are sharing. If what you're sharing is pivotal in helping others make changes to their lives your 'true you' comes out to play. You learn how to dance to the tune of your audience; you seem to pluck information out of some mysterious place of knowledge, mainly because you let go of the focus on self. That's when magic happens. One of the best ways I know to identify an introvert or extrovert is to consider how they recharge when exhausted. Extroverts need company, whether that is a party or a cafe or simply visiting friends. An introvert prefers time alone or with a significant other.

Know who you are

Here's another way. Have you ever noticed you feel exhausted after spending time with a high-energy person? That's because extroverts take your energy (yes, they are energy vampires!) whereas introverts give energy. That explains why I need space after my high energy training sessions.

So introvert I am, and as the years fly by, staying in the comfort of my home creating courses, reading good books and having the odd glass of sparkling wine grows more appealing. How easy would it be just to disappear, to truly become invisible, to not read the paper or watch the news, to not be distressed about the state of our world today?

We can all contribute

However, something deeper than my self-interest wells up and pushes me onto the platform of life. Too easily, emotion catches my heart and tears spill over as I see the carnage and the suffering of fellow human beings. But what can I do?

What difference can 'little me' make?

The truth is, every significant movement has started with a single person. Every great change is the result of just one person having the courage to connect and finding the confidence to talk to others, to share their vision and enthusiasm.

Last year, I ran public seminars for women who were Over 50 STILL Fabulous. Having the energy of this group in one room was exhilarating. However, as I turned off the lights at the end of the last seminar, a realisation hit me. Next time, the lights had to be turned on to a difference audience: women who were a decade older.

There is an ulterior motive for doing that. You'll unravel it as the book unfolds.

I hope you'll want to be part of my ulterior motive. No need to be afraid, we are not talking about world domination, well not in the traditional sense anyway.

How to get the most out of this book

It makes sense to read this book following the five-part formula: From NOW to WOW. We start with NOW: an unveiling of your current situation then explore the different stages of your life through to part five: WOW! Read these parts in chronological order. It's important to look at where you are and what got you there. Only then can you understand how to move forward to live a life you'd prefer.

Each part has a carefully selected quote for you to reflect on. Please take a moment to do just that. These are the 'Women of Wisdom (WOW) quotes' sent out to my list of wonderful women. The quote for each part contributes to deepen your understanding of the following chapter. An aide memoire if you will.

Additionally, each chapter ends with a summary of key points and 'Rays of Light'. A bit of fun here, but think about it: one word can act as that ray of light, piercing the darkness. These 'Rays of Light' shine a light on each chapter's message in a clear, penetrating way. Sometimes to simply restate a point, other times to go deeper.

Highlight, Highlight, Highlight

This book is not meant to sit on your bookshelf in a pristine condition. My intention is for you to act on what you've identified will work for you. One way to do that is to mark your identified thoughts with a highlighter. Consider using one colour for the first read. Then, for each further read use a different colour highlighter. This is invaluable in showing how deeper layers of knowledge are revealed with each reading. You probably already do this.

As a smart, single woman over 60, I look back on my life's journey and marvel at how it's unfolded, with all the twists and turns and detours along the way. The tears, the jeers and the cheers are all part of my school of hard knocks, each helping to shape my character.

Just like you, I have many life experiences and learnings to share

My early childhood was an adventure of moving from country to farm to tent to island and back to the mainland. Therefore, it seems logical to conclude my reluctance to settle down and become a 'suburban housewife' was born of these wandering childhood years.

Like many 18-year-old Aussies, my wandering extended to a sea journey to the UK for a two-year working holiday. This journey enriched my young life with new sights, new cultures and new people. One of those 'new people' travelled back to Australia with me. Before long we were married. Ten years later, as a single parent raising two young children, life was indeed challenging. And those challenges grew as my children grew. But that's another book.

We are a powerful group

In Australia there will be more 60th birthdays this year than ever before. In six more years, one in five will be aged over 60. We are a powerful group with a strong voice. We can stand up and speak, each in our own way, because we can make a difference. Indeed, it is our moral duty to make that difference.

That difference can be simply standing taller and smiling as you share your stories, your accumulated wisdom, with those who will listen. They may be your grandchildren or the grandchildren of others. Knowing what you value in life and living those values makes a difference. Some women decide now is the time to get that degree they've always wanted. Others step up and learn how to tango. Volunteering abroad or closer to home to help those much less fortunate makes a difference. There are many ways, big and small, to make a difference. If you're unsure how you can make a difference, you won't be unsure by the end of this book.

We are the Elders of Our Time

As women over 60, I believe we are the 'Elders of Our Time'. An elder can be defined as a leader or influential senior figure in a tribe or other group; one worthy of dignity and respect. But is this

> "The real voyage of discovery consists not in seeking new landscapes, but in having new eyes."
> – Marcel Proust

how we see ourselves? Do we see ourselves as a burden or a benefit to society? Yes, it's true others may see us as a burden, well past our use-by-date. If we accept that judgement, then it will be so. When *we* value our contribution to our families, to society and the global community then we step into the reason for our being. Right here, right now.

I believe a joyful life is an individual creation that cannot be copied from a recipe. Although a generalisation, baby boomers prefer step-by-step recipe-like directions. This book offers those directions using my five-step formula From NOW to WOW. Even so, you must choose your own path as you step through each part and each chapter. Do not end up like those who feel their lives were wasted. Wringing wrinkled hands, they look back and remember only anxiety and boredom. It doesn't have to end like that. You have free will; you can choose how to respond to the ups and downs of life. As you well know, many are denied the privilege of celebrating their 60th birthday.

This book is a courageous endeavour inviting you to look at other roads to explore on your life's journey, to see with new eyes. Finally, I like who I am today and can stand and proudly say "I'm over 60 and still fabulous."

"It takes courage ... to endure
the sharp pains of self discovery
rather than choose to take
the dull pain of unconsciousness
that would last the rest of our lives."

-Marianne Williamson

www.Over60StillFabulous.com

PART ONE: NOW I'M HERE
MIRROR, MIRROR ON THE WALL

It's reality check time! Time to get clear on where you are right now.

Are you in the driver's seat or the passenger seat of your life's journey? Perhaps you've always preferred to sit in the back seat? Recently, a woman shared she felt like she was trapped in the boot! When is it time to step up and get into the driver's seat of your own life?

To truly do that, you need to make a decision: to take the Blue Pill or the Red Pill. If you too are a fan of The Matrix movies, the significance of this choice is obvious. The Blue Pill takes you back to your make-believe world, where you pretend to be happy and where it's okay to be denied significance. You choose to live in the blissful ignorance of illusion. And that's your right to do so! Taking the Blue Pill means you'll probably want to stop reading this book.

The Red Pill signifies embracing the (sometimes painful) truth of your reality. This book is about taking the Red Pill. Taking the Red Pill signals that you want to find the courage to look at the reality of your life. No journey can be planned and no destination reached if we don't know where we are right now.

PART ONE is here to establish who you are and what you feel right now. Some of it will be good, some will be distressing. Either way, you can't reflect on or change that which you don't recognise within yourself.

Are you ready? We're about to find out who you really are!

Chapter 1
Flushing Out Your Values

To make the best of life you must know what's important to you about life; not knowing what you value in life is like a boat without a rudder. Your journey will be aimless, going this way then that way. Our values guide our every decision and the satisfaction or violation of them can produce strong emotional reactions.

Your values help you live life on your terms

No one can tell you what to value in life. That decision belongs to you alone. I have values for both my business and personal life. These are my top three business values:

1. Integrity
2. Freedom
3. Abundance

Looking at my top value of 'integrity', this word represents a whole set of experiences and emotions that are mine alone. Your experiences of what you consider represents 'integrity' cannot be exactly the same as mine. Integrity, freedom and abundance are abstract words with a wide range of possible meanings. When using abstract words, we must clarify our meaning of them.

What are your values?

Discovering your values involves a step-by-step process.

The values process

As a rule of thumb, values can be written in one to three words. A variety of questions help you discover your values in life. This one is my favourite:

What's important to me about ___? (The blank space identifies the area to be explored.)

You may wish to drill down to discover your values in life categories such as social, family, personal development, spiritual matters and purpose. For now, we'll look at your whole life perspective.

Please read through the first part of this process before starting to write.

Sitting comfortably with pen and paper (or at your computer) get ready to answer a simple question. Proceed to write down whatever pops into your mind. Eventually, you'll come to a blank space. Because your mind is a 'blank', you'll think you've finished. Not true. Keep asking "What else is important to me about my life?" and you'll discover more to write. Again, you'll experience another blank space. Don't give up! Push through. Continue to ask and finally more will come. Although some brave souls push through three blank spaces, for now we will work through two blanks.

Ensuring you follow these directions, start the process by asking: What's important to me about my life?

Now write. Remember to push through two blank spaces.

Excellent! You have now identified a list of values important to your life. That list may contain words like love, children, parents, friends, helping others, holidays, being honest, health, vitality, and having connection. Or happiness, intelligence, family, laughter, grandchildren, wealth, acquiring more knowledge, agility, peace or finding security. Now you need to find out, from that list, what matters most to you.

What matters most to you?

The next step clarifies each value by ranking their order of importance. Asking the question "Of these values, which one do I consider most important?" helps achieve this. Working quickly down your list, mark the one you deem most important as number one. Mark the next most important as number two and so on until all values are prioritised. During this step, you may choose to eliminate some values. (More than ten values become unwieldy and unnecessary.)

Now look at your top three values. Are you surprised? If we don't know what we value in life, we struggle to design goals that have the best chance of working for us. If our goals don't conform to our true values, we sabotage ourselves, every single time. For instance, valuing 'freedom' may require starting your own business. However, if you also value 'security' and rank it higher than 'freedom' you have a conflict of values. This creates an extremely uncomfortable situation. As many new business startups will testify, if 'security' was a top value they would've stayed in their jobs. Thankfully for me, 'security' didn't even make my original list.

The Litmus Test question

Time to test the reality of your prioritised values list. This is the final part of the process to determine what you truly value. Some Neuro Linguistic Programming (NLP) practitioners call this 'The Squirm Question'.

Looking at your prioritised list, ask "If I can have my No. 1 value but NOT have my No. 2 value, would that be OK?" If your answer is "Yes!" then you have the correct order. But if your answer is "No!" then you must move your No. 2 value up into No. 1 position.

Let's illustrate using my business values. I'd always thought 'freedom' was my No. 1 value. However, asking the Litmus Test question revealed the truth. Although 'freedom' was important to me it was not important if I did not have 'integrity'. Without 'integrity', 'freedom' meant nothing. Therefore 'integrity' moved to No 1.

Having clarified your No. 1 value, now ask "If I can have No. 1 but NOT have No. 3, would that be OK?"

In my case that reads "If I could have 'integrity' but NOT have 'abundance', would that be OK?" My answer is "Yes!" because 'abundance' without 'integrity' means nothing.

Continue working down your list, comparing your No. 1 value to all the values below it. This will not take long. Remember, a list of more than ten is unnecessary. I completed this activity quickly because my list identified only my top five prioritised values.

The next step is to discover if our No. 2 value deserves to sit in that spot. Therefore, my question would be "If I could have 'freedom', but NOT have 'abundance', would that be OK?" This one seems a bit tougher to answer. Even so, my answer is "Yes!"

You may struggle with assessing the importance of a value. To gain clarity, consider swapping the values around. In my case, I would now ask "If I could have 'abundance' but NOT 'freedom' would that be OK?" For me, the answer is a resounding "No!" An example is a marriage where there is an abundance of material goods, yet a wasteland of love. Trapped in a loveless marriage, no matter how far you drive your Mercedes, is not freedom. Therefore for me, 'freedom' belongs at No. 2.

Continue working down your list, comparing your No. 2 value to all the values below. Then do the same for your No. 3 value and so on. You get the picture.

A final order soon emerges. Knowing what you truly value sets the compass needle. Knowing your true values means you will rarely drift off direction. Even when false promises and glittering objects attempt to lure you on another course. Do not be led astray. Stay true to your own values for they give you the greatest chance to find happiness.

Things and people change

We've noticed this on our journey through life, haven't we? What you once valued may no longer hold true. Discovering your values is the first step. Take the time to reassess every now and again. Values and beliefs are intimately linked to each other. This reassessment challenges and liberates you from beliefs that do not belong to you. To find out more, a simple Google search using the NLP keywords 'eliciting values' will bring you tons of information and processes. Do the search; have fun.

Flushing out your values is the first chapter of this book for a very good reason.

As you work through each part, you may make changes to how you perceive life. It will be useful to reflect on whether or not your values have changed. At the end of this book, I've asked you to do this values exercise again. You may be surprised at the shift if there is one. When you embrace what you truly value, only then can real change occur.

<u>NOW</u> Chapter 1:
Flushing Out Your Values – Three Rays of Light

1. What are your top three values?
2. Workshop the values question around another life category: What's important to me about ___? (My relationships, family, friends, career ...)
3. Knowing your values clears the clutter of confusion. This example shows how. You're excited! Uncovering your true value of 'freedom' supports your cherished goal of starting your own business. Unfortunately, no matter what you do things go badly. Eventually, finding another job seems the only option. You feel like a failure. Further probing may've uncovered you value 'security' higher than 'freedom'. It now makes sense. A new business provides little sense of security. Your bold new venture was doomed from the start because of your strong value in security.

Identify Your Ray of Light: take a moment to write down what you got from this chapter.

Summary

- Your values help you live life on your terms.
- Use the values process to determine your true values:
  » What's important to me about ___?
  » Of these values, which one do I consider most important?
  » The Litmus Test question - If I could have (No. 1 value) but NOT have (No. 2 value) would that be OK?
- Don't be worried if your values change over time, they will.

Chapter 2

The Stranger Staring Back

I well remember the day it happened.

Standing at my bathroom mirror, someone I didn't know was staring right back. A stranger in my bathroom! What trickery was this? Surely that woman couldn't be me. Look at those bags under her eyes, those deep lines etched into her face and those brittle strands of grey hair refusing to be smoothed down. One thing shocked me even more. This stranger's eyes were dull and lifeless and they were staring right back at me.

Yes, I remember that day well, the day I truly saw myself in the mirror.

Who's there?

So, did I suddenly age overnight? How come I'd not noticed the bags, lines and grey hairs before this day? Apart from refusing to see them, the reason is clear.

Let's say we only look in a mirror three times a day (although it would be more). On average, that means we've seen our reflection around 657,000 times by the time we've turned 60, so how can I say we don't truly 'see' our image? Because when we look in the mirror, all we see is what needs fixing. This need could be applying lipstick or foundation or plucking those unruly eyebrows and shaping our hair. Or simply checking to see if we have parsley wedged in our teeth (because no one ever tells you about the parsley).

We glance at ourselves in the shop window as we walk by, but not to congratulate ourselves on our choice of outfit. No, we notice our bottom drooping down or our tummy sticking out or our hair sticking up or a myriad other things that are not quite right; so familiar feelings of not being good enough creep in. And that 'not being good enough' further affects our posture, our smile and our eyes as we step forward and introduce ourselves to that new person in our life. This could be our new boss or the first meeting with a romantic interest or a new prospective daughter-in-law or your bank manager. The issue is this; no matter who they are, at some level, they will pick up how you feel about yourself. And that's how they will relate to you. This then further cements your fears about not being good enough.

But what made this day different?

As I stood in front of my bathroom mirror, judging my reflection, I couldn't help but wonder what made this day different? Why am I noticing my true reflection today?

Oh by the way, I should warn you of a character trait of mine, which some find very annoying. I always wonder why a thing is so, why an event turned out the way it did, why people do what they do; the list goes on. This intense curiosity has turned out to be an incredible asset because it means life is rarely boring. When one is always asking, "Why is it so?" there are new discoveries to be made, exciting ideas to take on board and an opportunity to understand the many mysteries of life. It's a shame few seem to appreciate my gift.

I never did figure out why that day was different, but I did work out why I needed to acknowledge the stranger staring back.

Have you ever truly looked at yourself in the mirror?

This means not criticising or judging what you see as not being good enough.

Here is a simple activity I encourage you to do. Read the next paragraph then put this book down and go do it.

Stand in front of a mirror and look deep into your eyes. Breathe slowly and deeply; relax. Do this for five minutes (yes, five minutes). Notice what happens.

Welcome back. What happened? Perhaps nothing, apart from feeling ridiculous and noticing how long five minutes is? However, if you lasted the whole five minutes, did you feel strong emotion start to rise? When I did this, tears welled up and rolled down my cheeks. I don't know why, except to say it was like lifting the many veils shrouding the self. Others describe this experience as peeling back the layers of an onion, some talk about taking off the mask. For me, the tears were in recognition of a connection I'd not felt for a long, long time. A connection that went much deeper than the visual. It was a beautiful and grounding experience of re-connection with that stranger in the mirror. It was a realisation those 'dull and lifeless' eyes actually sparkle and shine when engaging with others. It was the realisation my visual appearance was not my true identity.

What is your true identity?

My true identity involves more than wanting to look and feel 20 years younger, of being caught up in our society's obsessive adoration of youth. Continuing to look in the mirror, I see a woman moulded by genetic programming, culture, society, family and friends. I see a woman who wants to be loved and accepted. This woman remembers the vibrancy, the spontaneity, the dreams and the daring to live life her way. I see a woman who wonders at how quickly the years have sped by, who has lost count of the many veils needed to hide her true identity.

Why do we hide our true identity?

Over the years, the most common answer has been the fear of non-acceptance. The fear that who we really are will not be deemed as good enough by those we know and love. So we live a lie, pretending to be who we're not and spend our days hiding our true 'unworthy' identity.

As women over 60, we've seen a bit of life right? We've been there, done that. We've learnt the rules of society, been tamed by our family dynamics (or not) and had our fair share of drama and pain. The many twists and turns of our life's journey may have brought happiness or created a longing for that 'missing something'. Perhaps we remember little of life's details, especially from our younger years, but even if we could, would those memories be a true rendition of what truly happened? That's most unlikely.

The stories we tell ourselves

Looking in the mirror, do we see opportunities lost, challenges avoided, love denied? We all have stories we tell ourselves, and others, about our past. Often these stories paint a dark picture of resentment and dismay for the path we chose along the way. I believe we can change those stories. Who knows how true they are anyway. What if we did that? What if we went back, way back to review the timeline of our life? With our wisdom and experience as women over 60, how could we interpret events differently? What would we see now that we were blind to before?

Our stories reveal where we live

As I look back on my life and my many sad stories, one thing is painfully clear. Regardless of my true physical address, I've always lived on 'The Island of Lack'. Sadly, I've discovered thousands of other women live there too.

Take a moment to revisit your life stories. Do they talk about the many 'lacks' you've experienced in your life? Do your stories talk about the many things you wished you'd had or done or been? When you get in your car, do you tune into the same old 'my sad story' radio station? Well I'm here to tell you there's never been a better time to live a better life. To do that though, we need to understand where we are and how we got here.

Why go back to where we began?

Why? So we're not seduced into taking the same turns, side streets and detours we've taken before and suddenly finding ourselves in the same fine mess.

If we looked at our personal stories in terms of 'lack', how many 'lacks' are there? The only true answer is 'lots'. But how can we tackle lots without going into overwhelm? From countless women sharing their stories over the years plus my own experiences, the main issues became clear. We can create a better life by addressing just three core issues of lack:

1. Lack of courage
2. Lack of confidence
3. Lack of celebration

Are these three 'lacks' the main themes of your stories? Imagine how different your life would be without the restraint of these three 'lacks'?

By the way, am I saying you've never been courageous or confident or had fun? Absolutely not! Of course you've expressed and exhibited those traits and behaviours, especially in your younger years. What I am saying is, even though we are women over 60, we choose *not* to rock the boat. We choose *not* to speak our truth, deciding to say something nice instead. We choose to deny our own needs to keep the peace. We eventually wither away, becoming little old ladies.

I believe life is more than this

It's never too late to consider a new story, to rewrite the chapters of your life, to get back into the driver's seat. I don't live on 'The Island of Lack' anymore and am much happier with my new address, 'The Island of More'. This island is not about more money, more clothes, more shoes and bags, more holidays, more jewellery, more investment properties, more cars or more material things. As you know, one can have all these things and still live on 'The Island of Lack'. If you relentlessly focus on unpaid bills, past hurts, sickness, being hard done by, uncaring kids and the inconveniently bad weather, no matter how much money you possess you are poor.

Living with more happiness

Living on the 'Island of More' means choosing to live with more happiness. Twenty-three hundred years ago, Aristotle said that more than anything else men and women seek happiness. Looking at our consumer driven society of today, more 'stuff' does not guarantee happiness. I agree we can be happy in that hot flush of new stuff, but have you noticed how quickly it wears off? All these things are valued because we believe they will make us happy.

And happiness does not just happen. Personal development courses identify happiness as an emotional state we alone control. Yes, happiness requires control of our inner experience. Mastering that control becomes a necessary part of our life's journey.

You are invited to share that journey with me, to discover what it means to live on 'The Island of More'. Adopting an attitude of gratitude means recognising how rich our lives already are. Be thankful for what you have; you'll end up having more. But before we do that, we must dive deep into why we continue to live a life of 'lack'. If you concentrate on what you don't have, you will never, ever have enough. We must ask why we've let others drive our lives, why we've allowed ourselves to be 'under the influence'.

> # Do not put the key to your happiness in someone else's pocket.

It's time to find the courage and the confidence to speak your truth. After all, if we can't do that now, as women over 60, when can we?

"Without death, time would not be precious." – Alexander Green

When is it the right time to decide to live before you die? If that sounds harsh to you, then this book isn't for you. The definition of 'Tough Love': straight talking from my heart to your heart. I hope you decide to continue this journey with me.

Your time is precious; spend it well.

NOW Chapter 2:
The Stranger Staring Back – Three Rays of Light

1. Do the five-minute 'staring into your eyes' activity. There is no right or wrong result; only *your* result matters. Please take the time to do this. I promise you'll discover something you don't know now. Even if you don't last the full five minutes, that's still a result. If you're not used to asking WHY ... use this experience as a good reason to start.

2. Admit it: you talk to yourself often. What stories do you tell yourself? What stories do you tell others? If you feel sad, miserable, fearful or just plain old angry, I guarantee the stories you tell yourself will have 'lack' as the theme. Do you lack the courage and the confidence to change your stories? Is it okay to have celebration in your life? If not why not, who says it's not okay? Hint: probably not your friends or your children.

3. Decide to live before you die. Yes, that is a ray of light. Only you can make this decision. Decide to get into the driver's seat of your own life. Lying on your deathbed and regretting your life's journey is not the best destination.

Identify Your Ray of Light: take a moment to write down what you got from this chapter:

Summary

- Take the five minute look in the mirror at who you are.
- We hide our identity because we think it's not good enough.
- We all have stories about the past, but we can change how we paint those stories.
- If you live on the 'Island of Lack', don't worry, you can decide to move.
- The three common areas of lack are courage, confidence and celebration.
- Living with more doesn't mean material goods, it means more happiness.
- The time to decide to live is now.

Chapter 3

Why The Rear-View Mirror Is So Small

L et's continue with our mirror theme.

Here you are, driving along in a hurry to get to your destination on time. You occasionally glance up at the rear-view mirror, but your main focus is looking through the front windscreen of your car, which is as it should be. After all, how can you get to your destination if you aren't looking where you're going? How can you read the road signs so you know when to turn? How can you see when the traffic lights turn red?

Makes sense huh? Speeding along and looking only in the rear-view mirror is a recipe for disaster. Of course it is – who would be so foolish? Do that and you will crash and burn.

Yet that's exactly how many of us live our lives

We speed through our days, always in a hurry to get to where we want to be and not noticing or appreciating where we are. The front windscreen is big because it has to show us where we are now and where we want to go. It helps us focus on this moment, to become aware of obstacles and dangers along the way; to assess the need to detour.

Distraction is dangerous. Speeding along, some choose to respond to that mobile call or that text message. Now our focus is not on where we're going. That moment of distraction could mean an eternity spent elsewhere. No one has come back from the dead to let us know where that eternity will be spent. But we do know you will no longer be looking through your front windscreen and you will not reach your planned destination. Not that day anyway.

Perhaps you are very good at not answering that call or that text message. You understand the clear and present danger. Perhaps, instead, you're inclined to look constantly into the rear-view mirror. You keep looking at what's behind you, at the past. That's not a good strategy either.

Living your life through the rear-view mirror

Think about how you currently live your life. If you're inclined to live your life through the rear-view mirror, you *will* crash and burn. Some women live their lives like that, constantly looking in the rear-view mirror, paying attention only to what has passed. Worrying about things that are done changes nothing except your internal tense state. Haven't we all experienced that tenseness? It's like having a rock sitting in the middle of your gut. Nasty. Constantly looking into the rear-view mirror means you don't see what's happening right now. You don't see the road ahead. You don't see the traffic lights turn red!

And that's why the rear-view mirror is so small

We are not meant to dwell on that tiny mirror, that reflection of what has passed. The landscape of our journey, as reflected in the rear-view mirror, simply shows us how far we have come.

The horror movie right there in my rear-view mirror

When driving at night, have you ever thought those headlights racing up behind resembled the eyes of a monster? No? Okay, indulge me here. It's dark, there's nothing to see, and I've driven for hours so naturally my mind wanders. What if that was a monster racing up to get me?

By the way, I avoid watching horror movies. But sometimes a scary scene sneaks up, and before I cover my eyes, I've seen the scary bit. That scene is then

> **Never forget, what you can be is more important than what you have been.**

re-lived, over and over. It turns out I'm pretty good at directing my own legendary horror stories in my mind. That scene becomes bigger and scarier, especially at night. Especially when I'm driving on a lonely country road.

Focus on the positives not the negatives

This is exactly what happens when some look back on their life's journey. They remember the bad bits and not the good bits. "Don't talk to me about the good bits." they say "There weren't any!" Really? Is this a case of only seeing the monster's eyes and not realising it's just a car? Then they embellish their monster story. It's now bigger and scarier. Poor me, we say. Nothing good ever happens to me. Every reaction creates a result. What result do you prefer?

So decide to use the rear-view mirror as intended, a brief glance to check out where you've been, how far you've come and what is coming up from behind. The truth is, you can't drive into your future using the rear-view mirror.

NOW Chapter 3:
Why The Rear-view Mirror Is So Small –
Three Rays of Light

1. How much of *your* life do you spend looking into the rear-view mirror? Start to notice how you feel when you do that. Start to wonder why you do that. What benefit do you gain from doing that? There has to be a benefit, otherwise you wouldn't do it.

2. How many red lights have you driven through on your life's journey? When you constantly look to the past, you drag up the drama and the pain. The bonus is you get to feel bad all over again. You need to be right here, right now, in the driver's seat with your hands on the wheel and a clear destination in mind.

3. Do not be a belief thief. What someone once said to you was only an opinion; it was never a fact. Get a grip ... on that steering wheel and decide to turn into the street of Strength of Character. Or perhaps you prefer Sunshine Boulevard? Get back into the driver's seat and determine your own course in life.

Identify Your Ray of Light: take a moment to write down what you got from this chapter:

Summary

- Don't use the rear-view mirror to go forward.
- The past doesn't matter too much – that's why the rear mirror is so small.
- It can have an impact, so make sure you recognise any negative power and disperse it.
- What you can be is more important than what you have been.

Chapter 4

What You See Is What You Get

Two years ago in Darwin, whilst training 'How to Deal With Difficult People' a woman stood up and shared this story with the group.

"I'm the CEO of (Government Department) and it's taken me 45 per cent of my time over the last six months to finally get my difficult employee in front of a judge. Yet, after hearing all the evidence, the judge dismissed the case. Because the submitted evidence pointed to only the negative aspects of the employee, the judge said I was building a case against the employee. I am outraged!"

After a brief pause, I asked her to describe some positive aspects of said employee. "There weren't any!" she responsed angrily.

It was pretty clear to me, and the entire group, this CEO had a personality clash with her 'difficult' employee. Everyone has strengths. Every single person you know has qualities (yes, even *that* person).

You cannot see what you are blind to.

If all you do is focus on the bad, you will not see the good

One of my favourite YouTube videos is an interview with Alice Herz-Sommer who, until recently, was the oldest living Auschwitz survivor. Even with the horror of what she had been through in her lifetime, her simple strategy for living was "I know about the bad, but I look to the good." It's a beautiful interview and one you cannot watch without getting wet eyes. For me, it reaffirms the strength of the human spirit. You might want to check it out too.

"Be thankful for what you have; you'll end up having more. If you concentrate on what you don't have, you will never, ever have enough." – Oprah Winfrey

Assumption is another misdirection in life

You've probably heard this saying: assuming makes an ASS-U-ME. Yet, we assume every single day. Assuming is just another way of pretending we can read minds. How's that working for you? Have you ever been wrong after assuming something? Perhaps I should ask if you've ever been right?

So you're a good judge of character?

Often we assume we have the uncanny ability to sum people up instantly. Whether we admit this or not, it's a human tendency to label people. If we become more mindful of our thoughts, we would see how often we do this.

We also assume our immediate assessment of them is valid. Let's look at a typical scenario in a workplace environment. Can you remember a time when a new employee was introduced to the team? Instantly, you made an assessment of that person and deep in the depths of your internal filing cabinet, they were filed away under the appropriate label. That label might read 'Cocky', 'Confident', 'Arrogant', 'Lazy', 'Bad Breath', 'Fish Handshake' or any number of different ways to categorise your first impression of them.

Once we've made that assessment, once we've labelled them, it takes a lot for us to change that label. Mainly because we don't like it when our intuitive gut feeling is proven wrong. This situation applies to any situation we find ourselves in, not just the workplace.

Let's look to an example from my Leadership workshops.

Having tested this activity with thousands of supervisors, team leaders and managers, I can confidently share the surprising result with you. This is the scenario posed to the groups:

You have a team member you've decided is lazy

She really is lazy; you've had ample proof to justify your assessment of her. One day, you're walking through the workplace and you see this 'lazy' team member actually working very hard. What is the immediate thought that pops into your mind?

If you were sitting in this session, how would you respond to that question?

Like always, there's rarely just one answer. Some people respond with "It's about time." or "I was wrong." However, the most common response by far is "She knew I was coming." Thinking "She knew I was coming" shows resistance to the possibility you may have misjudged this person.

Once you've put the 'lazy mask' on her, it'll take a lot for you to admit you were wrong. And if you are proven wrong, you'll always be on the lookout for her to slip up, to show her true colours. Finally proving you were right in the first place. And she'll sense that. Imagine the subterranean pressure this creates, especially within families.

Ah yes, especially within families. You would know the saying "Your daughter's your daughter all your life, your son's your son 'til he takes a wife." We all know someone who is deemed the wicked mother-in-law. Perhaps you're that someone?

Some people seem to walk around just waiting to be offended

Sometimes we work with them and sometimes our children marry them. Rarely is it our own children of course. Or us!

We need to be aware of the glasses we're wearing, are they rose-coloured or harsh-coloured? What is the truth of the situation? Until we're prepared to examine our view of the world, we'll always get the same results because we'll always respond in the same way.

An interesting experiment conducted in the classroom of a public elementary school in 1965 illustrates how devastating labels are.

'Pygmalion in The Classroom'

Teachers were told some children were 'Growth Spurters' based on their results in the (non-existent) Harvard Test of Inflected Acquisition.

The intention stood clear. To determine the degree (if any) to which changes in a teacher's expectations produced changes in student's achievements.

The result of this experiment provided further evidence that one's expectations of another's behaviour may come to serve as a self-fulfilling prophecy. Here is a review by James Rhem, the Executive Editor of the National Teaching and Learning Forum.

"Simply put, when teachers expect students to do well and show intellectual growth, they do; when teachers do not have such expectations, performance and growth are not so encouraged and may in fact be discouraged in a variety of ways."

If you want to know more about the experiment 'Pygmalion in The Classroom', simply Google the title. (Google is a verb now.)

"We can't be what you can't see."

Some time ago, a mother shared a story about her young son. As they were walking home after school one day, he told her he'd been put in the 'dumb side' of the classroom. The teacher hadn't made any announcement; the kids just knew they were sitting in the dumb side. The mother couldn't believe her son's story, so she never talked to the teacher. She regrets that now. Whether it was true or not, her son believed it. And that was the reality he lived which extended into and affected his early adult years.

People will always live up, or down, to your expectations

What about the expectations you set for yourself? What do you expect of life? I used to be proud of the fact that I always got by. No matter what disaster happened, I always knew I would get by. And that's exactly what happened in my life. I've only ever 'got by', always only enough to pay the bills and scrape by.

Finally, it is fitting to close this chapter with an insightful quote from a great leader, one who was an elder of his time:

"If you are pained by external things, it is not they that disturb you, but your own judgement of them. And it is in your power to wipe out that judgement now." – Marcus Aurelius, Roman Emperor, Stoic Philosopher, 121-180 AD

<u>NOW</u> Chapter 4:
What You See Is What You Get –
Three Rays of Light

1. If you only focus on the things you consider bad in your situation, or with the world, that's all you'll see. You will be blind to the good. There are good things in our world today; you just have to look for them. And that's how it works with noticing the good about your own life as well.

2. Everyone has, at the very least, one strength. What if you decided to focus on that one strength? Perhaps start with someone you deem to be a difficult person. Perhaps start with yourself?

3. What expectations do you have of yourself? How's your scorecard going? Many women set high expectations, yet rarely congratulate themselves for achieving them. Rather they focus on when they don't meet those expectations and beat themselves up for that 'lack'. Then as a bonus, your inner critic reminds you of all those 'lacks' in your character. Isn't it true we are our own worst enemies?

Identify Your Ray of Light: take a moment to write down what you got from this chapter:

_____

_____

Summary

- Look to the good, even though you know about the bad.
- The other complete waste of time is to ass-u-me.
- Our initial assumptions are often wrong but we resist acknowledging that is so.
- Labels are hard to dislodge once you've slapped one on someone, so make the effort not to do so.
- Remember the Pygmalion experiment that proved how a prophecy (assumption) about someone can be self-fulfilling.

Chapter 5

My Tape Measure Has Shrunk And Other Lies

Have you ever bought a defective tape measure? You, like many women, probably use scales to gauge the effectiveness of your weight control routine. I've always used a tape measure because I've never trusted scales. Here's why. Every Army Reservist soldier must pass fitness and combat assessments. Carrying weapons and marching long distances with a heavy backpack certainly builds one's stamina and develops muscle. So jumping on the scales was scary, because everyone knows muscle weighs more than fat right? So that's why I always relied on that moment of truth revealed by a tape measure.

My tape measure never lied

Until recently that is.

According to my defective tape measure, something nasty was happening to my body, a most unattractive thickening of the waistline.

Desperate measures were called for, so out came the sewing machine to make what I called 'fat dresses'. As a rule, my weight tends to fluctuate. However, if it went up, it always came back down. Well, it used to always come back down. It is certainly a wake-up call when you can no longer fit into your fat dresses.

Recently, an image of a white hamburger bun with the heading "Wheat Tummy' dramatically turned up the volume of that wake-up call. That white 'muffin top' hamburger bun image looked exactly how my stomach looked when I wasn't trying to hold it in. I was gutted (excuse the pun).

So, should I accept this happens when one ages and get my sewing machine out to make up 'super-size fat dresses'? That's certainly an option. How easy would it be to simply sit back, relax and pour another glass of sparkling wine whilst reaching for another block of chocolate? I could say to myself it's okay; this is what happens when one ages. It's not my fault! I could let this 'fact' settle in and then reach for another glass of sparkling wine. Yes, that's an option, but I didn't want that to be my reality.

We make decisions every single day

The consequences of those decisions create our future. Consequences can be good for us or not so good. Deciding you can't be bothered to exercise today has a clear consequence. Eating chocolate and pouring another glass of sparkling wine also has clear consequences. "Oh, just this once" we say "it won't hurt!" The 'just this once' lie can easily lead to habitual behaviours that don't serve us. Life does not happen to us, it happens through us, through the decisions we make. Never give away your power to say yes or say no. Own your decisions, don't point the finger of blame at someone or something else. Enjoy that glass of sparkling wine I say; don't beat yourself up over having it. But don't lie to yourself about why you made that decision to do so.

It's pretty clear why I've developed my 'middle-aged spread' and it has little to do with my age and a lot to do with the daily decisions I make.

I just can't be bothered

During a recent coaching session, Jane often muttered "I just can't be bothered." She was astonished when she heard how many times she'd said it (yes, I counted). Jane was totally unaware of this habitual response, but quickly realised the negative impact on her life. If you keep telling yourself you can't be bothered, you won't be. Additionally, how do you think that will impact others when they hear you can't be bothered?

Time to confess here. Due to my army training, I've been disciplined to accept daily exercise. Recently though, when the time came to put on the runners these words tumbled out of my mouth "I just can't be bothered." When these five words were uttered, my body physically slumped down and felt weaker. The result? No exercise of course! And it was easy to justify that decision by finding something else much more important to do. Try it yourself if you don't believe me. Words are powerful and we can be careless with the ones we choose.

A doctor needed to deliver a powerful message to her patient. "What fits your busy schedule better, exercising one hour a day or being dead 24 hours a day?"

The power of words and water

You may be familiar with Dr Masaru Emoto's experiments with water. Dr Emoto found that exposing water to loving words produced brilliant, complex and colourful snowflake patterns. In contrast, water exposed to negative thoughts formed incomplete asymmetrical patterns with dull colours.

(I recommend his book *The Hidden Messages in Water.*)

Up to 75% of the human body is comprised of water

(According to H.H. Mitchell, Journal of Biological Chemistry 158, the brain and heart are composed of 73% water, and the lungs are about 83% water. The skin contains 64% water, muscles and kidneys are 79%, and even the bones are watery at 31%.)

Considering Dr Masaru Emoto's documented effect of words on water, what are we doing to our own bodies with our choice of words? Be careful what you say to yourself because you are listening.

To speak what you seek, you need to know what you want out of life. Notice the words you habitually use, do they support the life you seek?

Speak What You Seek.

I've heard women say "No one loves me." No one in the whole world? Does this mean you don't love yourself? Not loving yourself is a tough task for baby boomers.

A good example of the power of our spoken word is how we talk about the weather. It's winter and winter days have expected characteristics like cold, wind, rain, snow and storms. How often have you heard people say, "It's a miserable day"? Really? What do those words do to how you feel? Miserable right? Instead of stating the obvious, what if we focused on something to be grateful for? Now you may be a summer person and think there's nothing to be grateful for on a winter's day. That's your choice, but is it a choice that works for your well-being? I may be irritatingly positive, but I believe there is always something to be grateful for. You have free will. If you choose to have a miserable day experience, please don't share the doom and gloom with others.

Sitting in the driver's seat of your life's journey means under-standing the power of the words you choose. Choose wisely. Choose to speak what you seek.

<u>NOW</u> Chapter 5:
My Tape Measure Has Shrunk And Other Lies –
Three Rays of Light

1. What lies do you tell yourself? Do they sound like: "Just one more drink won't hurt" or maybe "I'll go on a diet tomorrow" or even "I've never hurt anyone."

2. Are you aware of your habitual behaviours? That's actually a trick question; a habit is defined as behaviour you're unaware of. If you are aware, then it can't be a habit, it's a choice. So what are you choosing to do that doesn't work for you?

3. How do you respond when someone asks how you are? Have you noticed so many respond with "Not bad"? What does 'Not bad' mean? I shock people by saying "I'm fabulous." You may think this is weird. Somehow, even when I'm not feeling truly fabulous, saying this improves how I feel. Does your habitual response work for you? If not, change it.

Identify Your Ray of Light: take a moment to write down what you got from this chapter:

_____

_____

Summary

- Don't give in to the 'just this once' lie.
- Take responsibility for your decisions – whether they're good or bad – and don't blame others for the consequences.
- Be aware of the power of words in relation to the effect on yourself.
- Focus on something to be grateful for.

Chapter 6

I'm Invisible: Does That Mean I'm A Super Hero?

I love golf. Sadly I haven't played for about ten years. But this year is the year my golf clubs will finally see some action. It was on a golf course, whilst searching for another wayward golf ball, I first heard a woman say "I feel like I'm invisible."

This happened a long time ago, but I still remember asking Mary what she meant. How could she be invisible? Chuckling to myself I wondered if she was a super hero in hiding under those unattractive golf shorts women had to wear back then. (Playing golf does strange things to your thoughts as one constantly wanders into the rough to find another wayward golf ball.)

Hey, it's my turn

With a sad look of resignation on her face, Mary described times when she'd be standing at a counter waiting to be served. And that's exactly what happened, a lot of waiting. Even though it was her turn to be served next, she rarely was. If there was a male waiting, he got served first, if there was a younger woman waiting, she got served first until Mary was finally asked "Can I help you?"

Mary did not say out loud "Well yes, you can serve me, it's my turn!" But that's what she was shouting inside her head. Because she was feeling resentful, her face showed that emotion. Mary's tone of voice also reflected her dissatisfaction. When Mary left, the shop assistant may well have said to her colleague "She's a grumpy old woman."

Perhaps the next time Mary stood waiting at the counter, that assistant avoided serving her. Few people have the courage or the confidence to deal with someone who is perceived as a difficult person. And so the vicious circle turns.

Cause and effect: the chicken or the egg?

Is it fair to blame the people behind the counter? Perhaps it is, partly. Good customer service policies advise staff to ask loudly "Who's next?" And yes, there'll always be one who has no understanding of what 'next' means. They'll be righteously thinking "That would be me." Then jump the queue, failing to notice disdainful looks.

What if Mary confidently said "I'm next"? Not in an aggressive way, in an assertive way. Interestingly, many participants in my workshops are not clear on what assertive communication is, especially women. Women can be accused of being aggressive when they're using an assertive communication style. Often, the ones who are accusing them of being aggressive (or as some would say, being bitchy) are other women. Sigh.

A wonderful way to describe assertive communication

SAY WHAT YOU MEAN
MEAN WHAT YOU SAY
WITHOUT BEING MEAN WHEN YOU SAY IT

The author of this formula is unknown, but I thank them for providing such a clever formula for clearly defining assertive communication.

As an important part of not joining the ranks of invisible people, let's look at what this formula means.

SAY WHAT YOU MEAN: Have you ever had a 'meaningful' meeting with someone, whether at work or in your private life, and left without any clue as to what that meeting was about? Many people soft pedal when there are tough talks to be tackled.

I can tell you that no one, and I mean no one (unless they're psychotic) truly likes conflict. Most people avoid it or handle conflict situations badly. So when you have something to say, simply say it. Don't put up with a situation you don't like or are uncomfortable with. If you pretend the situation isn't important when it is, you will end up finally spitting something out when you're angry or resentful. Not a good strategy, because that's when your message is rightly interpreted as aggressive.

Step up, don't fluff

So step up and find the courage to say what you mean, don't fluff or pussyfoot around. If you're scared to do this, please examine what scares you. You deserve to be heard, but you won't be heard if you don't step up and speak.

MEAN WHAT YOU SAY: Have you ever been called a nag? Constant nagging, also known as harping, diminishes the strength and value of any message. We know this, so why do we do it? The main reason is we don't feel heard.

If you feel the need to repeat yourself over and over because no one is listening, this causes you to feel worthless. In this instance, if you truly mean what you say, you will use different words, a different tone and hold your body in a different way. Non-verbal communication, such as thin lips or clenched fists, will be interpreted as aggressive. Sadly, you will be totally unaware you're doing this, but you're the only one who is.

When you mean what you say, they know

When handling the consequences of continued bad behaviour, there has to be an understanding that you mean what you say. Did your mum ever threaten you with being grounded or not getting this week's pocket money, but then relented? Threatened consequences must be carried out. Otherwise it's all just hot air. So you got away with your bad behaviour, but you didn't learn a valuable lesson. As a mother of young children, saying yes seemed the easy option. It was much harder saying no and not relenting, even through the tantrums. I grew up with the belief your word is your bond. Even if you believe there's little evidence of that these days, it's still a good maxim to live by. In the short term, giving in does seem the easy option. However, when you relent, when you give in, you're saying your word does not matter. There's a price to pay for this lack in strength of character. When your message is ignored, you might as well be invisible. We train people how to treat us.

WITHOUT BEING MEAN WHEN YOU SAY IT: The minute you are mean when you say it, then you are being aggressive. Any anger, resentment, hurt or other dark emotion will cloak the tone of your words.

Assertive communication is when you can talk about an issue in a calm, clear way with the intent of listening to understand. Notice if you're listening with the intent to reply. If you are, you're not really listening; it is not possible to do so.

Take off that Cloak of Invisibility

Have you ever gone home and said "Gee they were a grumpy lot today"? Consider this: grumpy face meets happy face, which face wins? Most people say happy face, but you know that's not true. A grumpy face will always crumple a happy face. If you've ever muttered about how grumpy every one was that day, go and look in the mirror. Perhaps the grumpy face is you?

I believe everyone has a beautiful smile

Yes you do too. A smile is a charming and powerful way to connect with people. An authentic smile can instantly create rapport. Now, I'm not saying go around with an insane smile on your face all day: that scares people. Smiling is a gift to give, yet is often withheld. Oh people will smile, but with lips clenched tight. That's not a smile; it's a grin. Grins suffer from misinterpretation much more than smiles do. Somehow, a grin can look smug or convey an expression of one-upmanship. Additionally, polite grins are often used to convey an air of superiority. Grin or grimace? Hard to tell sometimes.

A true, authentic smile has to show some teeth. Now, that's where the problem may be. As we age, our teeth tend to look grey or yellow. If you look in the mirror only to lament your yellow or grey teeth, then do something about it. Believe it or not, that's why some women don't smile. I've certainly noticed, since turning 60, my teeth were starting to look a most unattractive grey. I did something about that. If you don't like the colour of your teeth you can do something, and it's not overly expensive.

Have you ever been somewhere talking to someone displaying fashionably uber-white, perfect teeth when some idiot decides to take your photo? Smile they say. Horrified, all you can think about is your grey teeth. So you give your best grin, a pale imitation of 'the best smile in the world' standing right next to you. Sighing, you grit your teeth determining never to look at the offending image.

A genuine smile is a beautiful thing. And you cannot be invisible when you smile.

NOW Chapter 6:
I'm Invisible: Does That Mean I'm A Super Hero – Three Rays of Light

1. Have you ever heard yourself say "I'm invisible"? Why did you say that?
2. It's perfectly okay to communicate assertively. Notice when you miss the opportunity to communicate assertively. Write down what you could've said using the formula:
   SAY WHAT YOU MEAN
   MEAN WHAT YOU SAY
   WITHOUT BEING MEAN WHEN YOU SAY IT
   For the next five days, practise writing out all missed opportunities.
3. A grin has its place in our lives; notice if that's all you do. If you are someone who doesn't like to smile, realise you're not using one of the most powerful rapport tools available. To smile or not to smile? If not, why not?

Identify Your Ray of Light: take a moment to write down what you got from this chapter:

Summary

- Women struggle to be appropriately assertive.
- You don't need to be invisible.
- Here's how to do it; say what you mean, mean what you say without being mean when you say it.
- No one likes conflict, but if you have something to say, say it.
- We train people how to treat us.
- You can do something about minor imperfections, such as grey teeth.
- A smile rather than a grin is a beautiful way to greet the world.

Chapter 7
I Can't Afford That!

How often do *you* say 'I can't afford that'?

I grew up in a working class family. My dad worked extremely hard to support five children and, as was common in those days, mum stayed home to look after us.

Dad died last year. He believed you worked hard and earnt your retirement, for then the rewards would come. Unfortunately, these rewards were sadly lacking in the latter years of his life. He certainly didn't die a wealthy man.

Not having enough money was always an issue in our home

Here are some of the comments I grew up with, comments that were imprinted on my understanding of the fabric of life:

- We can't afford that.
- A fool and his money are soon parted.
- Money does not grow on trees.
- I'd rather be poor and happy than rich and sad.

During my childhood and teenage years, messages marrying money with 'lack' were imprinted on my psyche. These messages implied people who did have money were drug runners and gangsters. You could not be a spiritual soul if you desired money. You must work hard and be considered a good person. That was how life worked. It worked that way because 'Money is the root of all evil'. Unfortunately, I believed that was true. Many years passed before I learnt the true saying.

"The Love of Money is the root of all evil."

And how many in our world today are in love?

Many things happen in our world that make no sense, until you look at them from this point of view; follow the money trail.

A few years ago, I sat in the audience listening to a passionate and most gifted speaker, Don Tolman. Don has spent most of his life searching for answers to how we can have good health and happiness. That was the first time I heard the expression 'Follow the money trail'. Many things are perplexing about our modern way of life. For instance, why were we told margarine is good for you and butter isn't? Recent studies have proved beyond doubt how bad margarine is and how vital butter is for a healthy body. Why was this lie perpetrated? Did someone make money out of this falsification? I think they did ... you will have your own examples of 'Follow the money trail'.

To further cloud the issue, in many religions the love of money is condemned as a sin. So consider this. What if, deep down inside, you have a belief that being rich marks you as a sinner? If this belief is hard at work in the background of your life, how tragic would your relationship with money be?

It's tragic because it means, no matter how hard you work, no matter if you did find that money tree, you would sabotage yourself and end up broke. It's an inevitable outcome. Few care to be considered a sinner or not worthy by their peers. So, with this mindset, you cannot hold the desire for immense riches in one hand and the desire to be considered a good and worthy person in the other. It would create cognitive dissonance, a most uncomfortable state indeed.

The logic gets even worse if you follow it to the next conclusion. If you are poor, if you are not cursed with the lust for gold and riches then you will be considered a righteous woman.

Don't laugh. Look around at your life right now. Do you have a lot of money? Good for you if you do. Many single women over 60, even if they do consider themselves to be smart, don't have sufficient money to live a reasonably comfortable and dignified life. This causes a sense of shame where 'I should've known better' becomes the self-admonishment.

Why do so many women over 60 have little wealth to command?

There are many, many reasons and we certainly can't cover them all here.

Let's go back to one of those sayings many baby boomers grew up with and see how seriously flawed it is:

I'd rather be poor and happy than rich and sad.

We're talking about just two options here: 'poor and happy' or 'rich and sad'. What about the other two options? What about 'poor and sad' or 'rich and happy'? Is it possible to be rich and happy? Of course it is, but in my formative years this possibility was never mentioned. I was blind to this as a probable reality.

Most people don't want to be sad or considered *not* a good person. Therefore, being rich was out of the question because that meant you were both sad and not a good person. So, if you wanted to be a good person and you wanted to be happy ... then the only option left was to be poor, and righteously so.

As ridiculous as this sounds now, you must question whether this belief, or one like it, is operating in the background of your consciousness. You will never create wealth if this is true.

> I'd rather be crying in a Mercedes than crying on a bike.

The definition of paucity is an amount that is less than what is needed or wanted.

For most of my life I've lived with a paucity consciousness, and it showed.

Here's the takeaway

If you do not have enough money in your life right now, it can only be because of the beliefs you have around what it means to have money. The expression 'filthy lucre' reveals a belief around money.

Let's try this money mind experiment. In a moment, I'm going to ask you to consider taking action on an instruction. Please do not immediately think you can't afford to do it. Let's pretend you can afford to do it.

As soon as you read the instruction, be aware of the first thought that will run through your mind. Okay, here are your instructions (remember, pretend you are in a position to do this):

Withdraw $1,000 cash from your bank account and carry this amount around with you in your purse.

Write here your first thought as you read this instruction.

_____

_____

My initial thought

Now I will share mine. The instant I read those words, this thought popped into my mind: "No! Someone will take it off me."

I was stunned. Reflecting on why I'd immediately think that, I realised that's a fear I've carried about money all my life. That someone will take it off me. After all, "A fool and his money are soon parted." Interesting huh?

When the share market crashes or the real estate market spirals down, I've caught myself thinking thank goodness I don't have shares or investment properties. The scary thing is; those thoughts justify my lack of money and validate my asset-less situation.

What's yours?

Other women have shared that their first thought is "I'll lose it." What was your first thought?

This simple exercise may reveal an important truth to you too. The reason why you don't have the money you deserve.

As a young single mum bringing up two children, I remember feelings of dread when walking to the letterbox at the front of my home.

The sick feeling of not having enough money to pay those inevitable bills twisted my gut. I hated feeling like that. So one day I made a decision to not dread the 'letterbox walk'. Whenever feelings of dread surfaced, threatening to overwhelm me, my mind shouted STOP! Whilst I didn't totally stop those feelings, I did greatly diminish their intensity. This may look funny, but holding your hand up and signalling 'STOP' helps too.

<u>NOW</u> Chapter 7:
I Can't Afford That! – Three Rays of Light

1. When you say or think "I can't afford that!" you create that reality. Instead, what if you said "How can I afford that?" This is an empowering question that causes you to decide whether you actually do want to swap your money for that item. If you decide you do, then you'll figure out how you can afford it. And I don't mean maxing out the credit card either.

2. Did you grow up hearing sayings supporting the lack of money, or the evil of money? If so, can you see how the foundation of your relationship with money was formed way back then and how it continues to shape your life? Awareness is the vital first step to change.

3. Please consider carrying around a significant amount of money. This will teach you more about your relationship to money than any book or seminar can.

Identify Your Ray of Light: take a moment to write down what you got from this chapter:

_____

_____

Summary

- 'I can't afford that!' needn't be your mantra for life.
- Money is not the root of all evil, love of money is.
- Being rich is not necessarily a bad thing even though our baby boomer upbringing implied it was.
- Thinking that riches equal sadness can lead to self-sabotaging our wealth generating capabilities.
- Consider the implications of what the money mind experiment showed you.
- Reduce the overwhelmed feeling by mentally saying 'STOP' when negative thoughts come along.

Chapter 8
The Burnt Chop Syndrome

Were you the one who always ate the burnt chop? Sometimes, as a young mum cooking chops or sausages for the family, I'd accidentally burn one. Naturally, that one went on my plate. After all, I was the one who burnt it.

These days, my friends know I have a preference for food to be well done. What I mean by that is 'please don't give me pale looking toast or sickly looking muffins'. Unless it has a distinctive golden to dark brown surface, I'm not interested in eating it. When ordering a muffin, I always ask for the burnt one, much to the waiter's indignation.

Time for a confession. I've even eaten toast that's burnt to a totally unhealthy charcoal crisp. Yes I know charcoal is cancer causing and just so wrong, on many levels. But I still do it.

Imagine my surprise upon reading there's a name for this dysfunctional behaviour. Yes! Apparently, 'The Burnt Chop Syndrome' is a uniquely Australian expression. Further surprises unfold upon reading what it means if you suffer from this malady.

Initially, the justification is 'I burnt it so I should eat it.' If you happen to like burnt chops, then no problem. Perhaps you even secretly burnt the chop on purpose? But if you don't like burnt chops, and you still place it on your plate, what is the message you are giving to yourself and to others?

The message to you might be: 'I will give myself the worst so my family can have the best.' But, the message to the family might be 'I am the least important person here and deserve the worst.'

Or you could just like burnt chops.

Or were you a martyr mum?

Reading a recent blog post, a woman described herself as a 'martyr mum'. She confessed to always showering last, just in case the hot water ran out, sitting in the most uncomfortable chair so her family could have the comfortable chairs and parking on the road so her family could use the driveway. One day after spending two hours in casualty with a painful eye, she returned home and had to almost beg for a cup of tea. Now she's wondering if she raised a bunch of self-absorbed adults or is she just terrible at voicing her own needs?

You know this isn't just about burnt chops don't you?

Have you ever reached for that last French Earl Grey teabag then thought 'That's my daughter's favourite tea. I'll leave it for her.' Your daughter lives on the other side of the country. Regardless, you decide to save it for when she next visits. So you reach for the 'good enough' tea bag. That makes sense, doesn't it? I don't think so.

Be clear about what you want

A friend told this story about her sister Jane, who'd just returned from a four-week holiday in Europe. Jane hoped one of her adult children would pick her up from the airport. However, in phrasing her request to her son She was mindful of his full-on work life. She told him it was okay if he wanted to sleep in instead of coming to pick her up. Her daughter got a similar caveat. You've guessed what happened. No one came to pick Jane up. Her son sent a text saying he would sleep in. Her daughter also had a good reason why she couldn't pick her mum up. Even though Jane realised she'd set up the situation herself, she still felt hurt none of her children came to pick her up. Feeling miffed, she hailed a taxi home.

The Burnt Chop Syndrome strikes again!

Have you realised where you might be acting like a martyr? Possibly in your workplace as well as your private life?

It's worth looking up a blog called 'The Burnt Chop Syndrome'. The writer identifies herself as 'B' Here is her 'burnt chop' explanation:

"The Burnt Chop Syndrome is a response to mothers putting themselves last, to the tendency to look at what we don't have rather than what we do, and is a way to share my willingness to laugh at my life. I mean, if you can't laugh at it all, what's the point."

According to Val Allan, a Naturopath recognised as the 'grandmother' of the industry in Western Australia, *"The inherent danger with this syndrome is that mothers, as the prime caregivers in most cases, have a duty of care to look after themselves better in order to fulfil the roles they have chosen. There are obvious times that mothers have to put themselves much further up the pecking order so they can do the best for their families."*

Rosalie Pattenden, a Melbourne-based clinical psychologist with Relationships Australia says *"Women still tend to see themselves as responsible for the emotional well-being of the family and as a result they look after everyone else first and keep the burnt chop for themselves."*

Theresa, author of the blog 'Alittlebirdmademe.com' shares a compelling 'Burnt Chop' story. *"I heard the stories about burnt chop syndrome (a very Australian phrase that signifies mothers eating the food that isn't perfect while serving up the good, perfectly cooked food to their children and partner) and just chuckled knowingly, because of course I eat the burnt chop. That is what mothers do. Right?"*

Theresa continues to write about her family and a particularly distressing event they endured, then finished with this paragraph: *"Today marks the day that I say no to the burnt chop. I am going to build a life that nourishes me, and fulfils me. I am going to stop being the selfless martyr. And after all these years of being told that I am a 'good mother' I am going to choose to be a more selfish mother, so that I can in fact start to be the great mother that my children deserve."*

And here is a father's take: *"I've just come across "Burnt Chop Syndrome", which I had no idea existed as a phrase for something I have observed for years with my own mum."*

Finally, Blogger Kristin Austin has applied the 'Burnt Chop Syndrome' to business. *"Are you so busy running around fixing other's problems that you forget to focus on getting what you want out of your business? Lots of business people do. Are you like those business owners who get so caught up in 'doing' everyday, being busy, solving other people's problems, that you forget to look after your own needs? Just as scientists have discovered too much burnt (charcoal) meat can be carcinogenic, the business version can have just as dire effects."*

The expression 'The Burnt Chop Syndrome' may have been coined in Australia, but the ramifications of serving yourself the burnt chop are global.

NOW Chapter 8:
The Burnt Chop Syndrome – Three Rays of Light

1. Whilst you may not be actually eating a real burnt chop, what is it you are putting up with that represents 'eating the burnt chop'?
2. Are you a martyr mum too? If so, how's that working for you?
3. Do you serve yourself the burnt chop?

Identify Your Ray of Light: take a moment to write down what you got from this chapter:

Summary

- Do you like the burnt chop, or do you simply accept it?
- Are you a martyr mum?
- Make a conscious decision to ask for what you want.
- Move yourself up the pecking order.

Chapter 9
Sixty And Single: Sad Or Serene?

For the last decade I've been plagued by one question, a question that seemed to fascinate both friends and family alike. Thankfully, only one little old Greek lady still asks: "**Have you got a man in your life yet?**"

I've always felt curiously torn about how to answer. Really, was it any of their business? There were times when I wanted to get mad at them for being inconsiderate enough to ask. Many times, deep down inside, a little voice asked a similar question "So, why haven't you got a man in your life Victoria?" To which I would respond to myself "Obviously, I lack the qualities the man of my dreams looks for." Finally, I realised this self-talk was a one-way street to the cul-de-sac called 'Lack of Self-Esteem'. Once you become aware of habitual thoughts and behaviours that deflate your worth, you can do something about them. Then if you continue to have these thoughts and behaviours, know it's your choice to do so. Habitual behaviour is that which you're not aware of. So, why would we choose to continue with destructive self-talk?

Your life is yours

To make matters worse, some married friends even thought it appropriate to ask,

"How's your sex life these days?" Many times I was close to responding I was pretty confident it was better than theirs!

Do people seriously think they're complimenting you when they say "I didn't think an attractive woman like you would have any trouble getting a man." You have to wonder what the subtext is with that one.

And how about this little gem "You should accept his proposal Victoria, you're not getting any younger."

You have your own little gems I'm sure.

Times have changed; we have choices

In my younger days, it was a given that one would leave school, get a job, get married, have children and live happily ever after with one's loving husband. That was the natural order of life back then. Other possibilities never entered my mind.

> Few seem to accept one can be perfectly single and perfectly happy.

Yet here I was, a divorced woman with two adult children, absolutely single and feeling absolutely fabulous about that. Although I must confess, it did take some time to accept and embrace my single state. Many single women over 60 have their own story to tell about their single state and what that means.

Last year, at a workshop held in Perth, one woman shared her story.

After many years of indecision, she'd finally decided to end her marriage. It had been a difficult and unhappy marriage and she was proud to have made the decision to move on with her life. Even so, she dreaded telling her Italian father. When she finally plucked up the courage to do so, he told her she would never find another man because she would now be thought of as 'damaged goods'.

As she told her story, the hurt she still felt at her father's response was palpable. Even so, she'd found the moral courage to break free from her pre-determined road map, and she was proud of that. It wouldn't be easy, but she knew it was vital to live by her own values, by her own rules.

As single women over 60 we have lived life, but how have we lived it? Have we developed our own code of conduct or have we taken on what is deemed best for us?

Have we been smart?

Are we still under the influence? And I'm not talking about substances here, illegal or otherwise. Are we still under the influence of what others have decided is best for us? Isn't it time to break free? We're grown up now, it's time to make our own choices. I love being single and over 60. The spontaneity, the freedom, the joy experienced is tangible and contributes to my epic sense of well-being.

Today I noticed a couple sitting at the next table. Their love and care for each other was clear to see. Their grey hair and lined faces mattered not. As they smiled into each other's eyes, I felt their love. Once, I would've been jealous of such a public display of affection. Today, I bathed in their delight with each other and did not feel diminished or not good enough.

Yes it's true, not that long ago I would've felt diminished by this display of tenderness and love. Feelings of isolation and sadness would've risen up and threatened to engulf me in self-pity. So I know what sad feels like, and I don't like how that emotion affects the quality of my life. It took a while, but finally I discovered my ability to choose my emotional state, and you can too.

Feeling serene is a preference. What do you choose, sad or serene?

Sixty and suddenly single, sadly

We all know women, as a rule, live longer than men. So yes, you may be suddenly single – sadly. Or perhaps you are one of those women who've been traded in for a younger model.

Regardless of the reason why you are 'suddenly single', it also seems you are 'suddenly friendless'. Or more specifically, 'suddenly married-friends-less'. Your married friends are still inviting people to their dinner parties, dining out or going to the movies but your name is no longer on their guest list. If you've never heard the 'your invitation's in the mail' scenario, then you've chosen your friends well.

Why does this happen?

If this has happened to you, I bet you still don't know why.

The reason we don't know why, is we don't actually ask. Instead we make up all sorts of stories in our head and not one of those stories supports our fragile self-esteem. As if our situation wasn't dark enough, we now plunge ourselves deeper into the dark pit of despair by fabricating fanciful story lines. Then we act as if they're true.

So what to do? Ask!

Time to introduce you to an astonishing book called *Women Don't Ask* written by Linda Babcock (a professor of Economics) and Sara Laschever (a journalist). Last year, whilst researching negotiation skills, this book became a valuable discovery. I describe it as astonishing because, prior to reading it, my mindset was one of not needing this guidance for myself. After all, I quite confidently ask for what I want. This book made it totally clear I was delusional on that subject. You will find this book covered in more detail in Part Four.

Back to why you are suddenly single and friend-less and what to do about that. Do you have the moral courage to ask your friends why? But, I hear you say, I shouldn't have to do that. If they were true friends, surely they'd understand and support me. Clearly this is not the case in so many situations. As most people are not mind readers, we're left to make up our own stories on why we are suddenly excluded.

What is my contribution to the situation?

Perhaps the first step is to reflect on this question. What is it I could be doing to create this situation? Be honest with your answers and write them down. Could it be your friends are embarrassed by the situation and don't know how to handle it or what to say to you? Does your friend fear her husband may want to be by your side instead of hers? Are you so deep in despair they can't handle the emotion? Perhaps their relationship is fragile and they're struggling to hold it together. So many possibilities and so few of them will be about you.

What if you decide not to ask questions of yourself or of your friends? Remember, the only person on this planet you can change is – yourself. You cannot change any other person, but you can influence them.

Whatever the reason for your suddenly single status, you cannot change the fact it's happened. Grieving is a personal matter. We all have our own way of dealing with death or abandonment. Some recover quite quickly; others need a much longer timeframe. Eventually, there comes a time when the protesting and moaning and groaning must stop. It's time to move on. If you don't move on, you'll be considered painful to be around because even the best of friends grow tired of never ending drama.

NOW Chapter 9:
Sixty And Single –
Sad Or Serene? Three Rays of Light

1. Do you have well-meaning family and friends who ask "Have you got a man in your life yet?" How do you feel when you hear this question? How do you respond?
2. Have you developed your own Moral Code of Conduct? Or are you still living under the influence of others?
3. Consider buying the book 'Women Don't Ask', even if you think you do ask.

Identify Your Ray of Light: take a moment to write down what you got from this chapter:

_____

_____

Summary

- Single? Choose to be serene.
- Reject the self-talk that leads to low self-esteem.
- Do something about habitual thoughts that deflate you.
- You can be perfectly single and perfectly happy.
- Understand the influences that guide you.
- You have the ability to choose your emotional state.
- After becoming single many women lose their married friends – you need to ask those friends why.
- Many reasons for people's behaviour will not actually be about you.
- The only behaviour you can change – is yours.

Chapter 10
Is This All There Is?

Have you ever woken up in the middle of the night and wondered what it's all been for? Life I mean. What has the purpose of your life been?

Have you made a difference? Have you left a legacy? When you're lying on your deathbed, what will you regret? Will you wish you had lived your life differently? When people are gathered around at your funeral, what will they say? If there are tears, will they be genuine or are they just there to hear the reading of the will?

Even though these questions might offend you, remember this is a book of 'Tough Love'. Yes, these are tough questions, especially if you have a fear of dying. However, better to reflect on your answers to these questions now, when you can still do something about them.

Throughout our lives, we get little nudges to show us we are not living how we'd prefer. Many of us live in denial, saying we are content, even happy yet deep inside the truth sits – rock solid in our gut.

I clearly remember one of those nudges and how it changed my life

Here I was again, in another airport waiting for another delayed flight home. A woman, who looked a bit older than me, caught my attention. She was slumped down in her seat clutching a glass of red wine as she stared out into the dark night. She caught my attention because she looked extremely sad and deeply lonely. Just like you, I'm good at mind reading the state others are experiencing.

But was she really sad? Perhaps she'd had more than one glass and was feeling a bit tipsy. Perhaps she was deep in thought. Whatever the truth of this scenario, it left a deep impression on me.

Later, sitting safely on the plane, I realised it was more likely a projection of my own feelings. On average, I'm on a plane two to seven times a week for 40 weeks of every year. On top of that, many nights are spent sitting in hotel rooms finalising training for the next few days. And I've been doing that for over six years now – it's a lonely life.

But I kept doing it

Sure, it was fun sometimes. I enjoy meeting new people and visiting new places. However, there comes a time to take accountability for your life's journey. To stop complaining and start planning how you'd prefer you life to be. Finally, I did just that. 'That' meant jumping off the edge. It meant leaving a safe, predictable place (also known

Fear is temporary.
Regret is forever.

as your comfort zone) and setting sail for uncharted waters. Here I go again, over 60 and acting like I'm only over 20.

Wanting to create a better life, creates that better life

Standing in your own power and deciding you are worth a better life creates that better life. I know that sounds a bit 'woo woo', but that's exactly my point. You would not have this book in your hands if I had not jumped off the edge.

No matter what's happened, do not blame others for the reality of your life. That only causes you to feel powerless. Get into the driver's seat, grab the steering wheel and get into gear. It's your journey. If you're not charting your journey, there's a huge price to pay. Do not wait until you're on your deathbed wishing you'd been braver and stronger, wishing you'd driven down a different road. Or taken a detour.

Even if you've seen this article before, now is a good time to review these insights.

Nurse reveals the top 5 regrets people make on their deathbed

For many years, Australian nurse Bronnie Ware worked in palliative care looking after those who had gone home to die. She was with them for the last three to twelve weeks of their lives. As expected, each patient experienced a variety of emotions, denial, fear, anger, remorse, more denial and eventually acceptance.

Bronnie was especially clear on this point *"Every single patient found their peace before they departed though, every one of them."*

Here are the five most common regrets her patients shared:

1. *I wish I'd had the courage to live a life true to myself, not the life others expected of me.* This was the most common regret of all. When you realise your life is almost over, it's easy to see how many dreams have not been fulfilled. Most people had not honoured even half their dreams and had to die knowing that it was due to choices they had made, or not made.

2. *I wish I didn't work so hard.* This came from every male patient she nursed. They realised they'd missed their children's youth and their partner's companionship. Women also spoke of this regret, but as most were from an older generation, many of her female patients had not been breadwinners. All the men Bronnie nursed deeply regretted spending so much of their lives on the treadmill of a work existence.

3. *I wish I'd had the courage to express my feelings.* Many people had suppressed their feelings in order to keep the peace. They'd settled for a mediocre existence, never becoming who they were truly capable of becoming. Many developed illnesses relating to the bitterness and resentment they carried as a result of this.

4. *I wish I'd stayed in touch with my friends.* Often they would not truly realise the benefits of old friends until their dying weeks and it was not always possible to track them down. In the end, all that remains is love and relationships.

5. *I wish I'd let myself be happier.* This was a surprisingly common one. Many did not realise, until the end, that happiness

is a choice. They'd stayed stuck in old patterns and habits. Fear of change had them pretending to others, and to themselves, they were content. But deep within, they'd longed to laugh properly and have silliness in their life again.

When you're on your deathbed, what others think of you is a long way from your mind. As Bronnie noted *"Health brings a freedom very few realise, until they no longer have it."*

If you would like to read more, check out Bronnie's full-length book *The Top Five Regrets of the Dying – A Life Transformed by the Dearly Departing.*

Perhaps some of these regrets struck home with you?

There has never been a better time to do something about that. Do not believe the saying "You can't teach an old dog new tricks." What rubbish!

The rest of this book will guide you on what you can do to make the best of the rest of your life. Let's continue our journey to understand why so many women have ended up in the passenger seat or the back seat of their own life.

NOW Chapter 10:
Is This All There Is? – Three Rays of Light

1. Write down five things you would like people to say about you at your funeral.
2. Have you ever 'jumped off the edge'? What did you learn? If you have never 'jumped off the edge' would you like to? What stops you?
3. Which, if any, of the top 5 regrets people make on their deathbed rang true for you? What is one thing you will change right now to prevent having that regret? Consider this: fear is temporary; regret is forever.

Identify Your Ray of Light: take a moment to write down what you got from this chapter:

_____

_____

Summary

- How will people remember you when you're gone?
- How we perceive others is more likely a projection of ourselves.
- Don't blame others for the reality of your life.
- The five common regrets of deathbed patients are:
  - » I wish I'd had the courage to live my life, not the life others expected.
  - » I wish I hadn't worked so hard.
  - » I wished I'd expressed my feelings more.
  - » I wish I'd stayed in touch with my friends.
  - » I wish I'd let myself be happier.

Chapter 11

This Is Your Life:
NOW I'M HERE

"You can't leave a footprint that lasts if you're always walking on tiptoe." – Marion Blakely

Where you are in your life right now?

Looking back on all we've covered so far and considering all those events and elements that have shaped your life to date, this chapter has to be written by you.

Please take the time to write down how you feel, what you're doing, what you'd like to do, what's missing and anything else that comes to mind.

Consider the following. Have you ever wanted to disown your reflection in the mirror? Do you spend too much time looking back on what has been? How are your expectations, or the expectations of others, influencing your life? Have you developed that middle-aged spread? Have you had the experience of being invisible? Does that matter? Have you always put yourself last? Are you sad or serene? Don't wait until you're lying on your deathbed to share regrets; identify one right now and make sure it will not be one when that time comes to pass.

The previous chapters have been a wake-up call, a reminder of how your life is or is not. No one else gets to see your words. This is your life ... so write:

_____

_____

_____

_____

_____

_____

_____

Please do not continue on to PART TWO until you've emptied your mind onto this page. It doesn't need to make sense, just do it! You may need to use extra sheets of paper. Keep writing until there is nothing more to write.

Finally, this space is for identifying just one thought from all you've written in Chapter 11. As you read through your own words, what is the most important, most compelling, most revealing thing you've written that jumps out and surprises or shocks you? It may be an uncomfortable truth. Delight in that, for designing a new life begins with awareness of the old.

"Out with the old, in with the True." – Jeff Brown

_____

_____

_____

_____

"And the day came
when the risk of remaining tightly
enclosed in the bud was more
painful than the risk it took
to bloom."

-Alicia Keys

PART TWO:
HOW I GOT HERE

Why am I travelling in the passenger seat, the back seat or even the boot on my life's journey? You've heard the expression 'Knowledge is Power'. Knowing how you got where you are today, what's caused you to choose those highways and byways, is the potent second step to creating a better life.

PART TWO highlights case studies on gender stereotyping. It identifies the consequence of being born female and delves into the resulting automatic behaviours. People aren't broken; they do what they do to get the result they do.

Then we look at why our comfort zone is a curse and why we seek approval. We explore why, even as adults, we don't speak our truth. Time to get acquainted with your survival strategy; you're the only one who hasn't seen it yet. The message is clear: you have the right to be who you really are.

Chapter 12

You Were Born Into A Pink World And Handed The Road Map For Your Life

Born female, your life's journey stretches out before you, meticulously mapped.

The second it's announced, "It's a girl" your world turned pink.

Into your newborn lap dropped the road map for your life, determined by both your parents and society. Each turn, each signpost, the high road or the low road, even those who will be your passengers, all predetermined. No provision is made for deviation or free will.

But what if you don't like the journey determined by others?

What if you choose to detour or turn left instead of right or linger longer or even decide on a different destination? For many, defiance incurs a harsh penalty. Depending on your family, your culture and the society you grew up in, that harsh penalty can range from an angry or silent parent to a death sentence.

And to complicate the scenario, what if you were born female but felt like a male inside? Or born male and felt female inside? Has that road map shaped or cloaked who you really are? Is gender the result of nurture or nature?

As always in matters like this, there is strong debate.

Totally opposite 'expert' opinions rage about nurture or nature. Here are some of those views:

1. Early in 2014, UK Consumer Affairs minister Jenny Willott said that women were being forced into professions that paid less well because of gender stereotyping when they were children.

2. Neuroscientist Prof. Gina Rippon, of Aston University, Birmingham, says gender differences emerge only through environmental factors and are not innate "The world is full of stereotypical attitudes and unconscious bias. It is full of the drip, drip, drip of the gendered environment." She believes that gender differences appear early in western societies and are based on traditional stereotypes of how boys and girls should behave and which toys they should play with.

3. Megan Perryman, who co-founded 'Let Toys Be Toys' a campaigning group against gender stereotyping, said "In our experience, children enjoy a range of toys and it's important they are encouraged to play with anything that interests them."

   According to Megan "Telling boys not to play at being caring, or girls to avoid toys involving science or physical activity can only serve to limit their potential. Children learn these 'rules' of how to be a boy or girl at a very young age, via marketing, media and those around them. It can be upsetting to the child if their interests do not conform and can prevent them from being the people they really are."

4. According to Neuroscientists Garcia-Falgueras and Swaab "Boys and girls behave in different ways and one of the stereotypical behavioural differences between them, often said to be forced upon them by upbringing and social environment, is their behaviour in play. Boys prefer to play with cars and balls, whereas girls prefer dolls.

   This sex difference in toy preference is present very early in life (3–8 months of age). The idea that it is not society that forces these choices upon children but a sex difference in the early development of their brains and behaviour is also supported by monkey behavioural studies. Alexander and Hines, who offered dolls, toy cars and balls to green Vervet monkeys found the female monkeys consistently chose the dolls and examined these ano-genitally, whereas the male monkeys were more interested in playing with the toy cars and with the ball. There is no indication that social environment after birth has an effect on gender identity or sexual orientation."

5. Jane's story supports the theory of these neuroscientists:

"I have a master's degree in gender research and I had to read more books on this topic than any other. I am also transgender so I know what it feels like to have a brain that is wired up female in a male body, though at university that statement was the source of constant debate. If my strong feelings of being female are the result of culture why did the constant male gender stereotyping I received at a boys school and from a very masculine father not correct this. I studied sciences 'til it was clear I was not going to become an engineer, I worked in a male dominated financial services industry, became a freemason, got married had children, engaged in countless psychological workshops to make me 'normal'. But nothing changed – I still felt as if I should have been a woman.

Eventually at 50 I gave in and began living as a woman. I have had some hormonal treatment but this is not about sex or relationships, it is about my sense of self – my gender identity – and that is female. Since I began publicly identifying as a woman 14 years ago I have never once regretted it, never felt the need to dress or identify as a man despite the discrimination. I have worked with gay, lesbian, bisexual, transgender and intersex people and researched their behavior and feelings. All tell me their sense of who they are, and especially their gender identity, was fixed from as long as they can remember and nothing has ever changed it. From my now extensive experience I am absolutely convinced that male and female brains are different – they are wired that way during fetal development and nothing we can do afterwards will make the slightest bit of difference. We are who we are."

6. Kate shared her own strong views in a blog post: "I believe there is nothing fundamentally 'female' about my mind. Just because I am female, doesn't mean I will be more similar in mind to another female than to a male. We are all different and we are all individual. I feel like I have a right to be recognised as individual and not to be stereotyped just based on my physicality."

So on one side of the court, we have neuroscientist Rippon, who claims male and female brains only differ because of the relentless 'drip, drip, drip' of gender stereotyping. On the other side, we have neuroscientists Garcia-Falgueras and Swaab who claim there is no indication that social environment after birth has an effect on gender identity or sexual orientation. The jury is still out on this one.

What matters most is your story and how your journey thus far has been affected by being born female into a pink world.

Were you a tomboy in your younger years? I certainly was. The label 'tomboy' was useful because it allowed acceptance of behaviour normally associated with boys. Because parents always think you'll grow out of it, they don't feel threatened. Then at age 29, I joined the Australian Army Reserve and became a soldier. Looking back on my life, it's easy to see why feeling feminine was a struggle. Perhaps I became a tomboy because it seemed boys enjoyed more freedom and adventure. Thankfully, I've finally fully claimed my right to be feminine.

The purpose of this chapter is to illustrate your right to be who you really are.

That probably sounds really weird when talking to women who are over 60. Shouldn't we already know it's okay to be who we really are?

Not according to the author of *Flow,* Mihaly Csikszentmihalyi. "Because we depend so much on the affection and approval of others, we are extremely vulnerable to how we are treated by them."

And we're not only talking about gender orientation here. Have you ever been placed in the position of being treated as the child whilst your children act as though they're the parents?

Can you sit down and have an honest conversation with your mother or your father or any member of your family? An 'honest conversation' means sharing your views on how family life unfolded, asking questions and seeking explanations. One reason this unburdening rarely happens is the fear of loss of affection and approval. Besides, each member of your family has their own story of what life was like 'way back then'. It's unlikely to be the same as your story, and we all believe our version is the right version. Right?

I was born into a pink world. My childhood adventures conspired to incorporate blue. Choosing to become a soldier, blue turned out to be my best colour. There were many good reasons why blue appeared more attractive. After all, don't they say "It's a man's world"?

<u>HOW</u> Chapter 12:
You Were Born Into A Pink World And Handed The Road Map For Your Life – Three Rays of Light

1. Can you remember instances of being stereotyped into your pink world? Thinking back to the time I landed my very first job, I told dad of my plans to save up to buy a car. That was 50 years ago, but his reply still rings clear: "Don't bother doing that. You'll get a boyfriend who has a car." So I didn't buy my first car until I was over 30. His words seemed to make so much sense, way back then.
2. Nurture or Nature? The experts certainly can't agree. What do you think?
3. Is Mihaly Csikszentmihalyi right? Are we vulnerable because we depend so much on the affection and approval of others?

Identify Your Ray of Light: take a moment to write down what you got from this chapter:

_____

_____

Summary

- Whose journey is it anyway?
- Nurture or Nature? Or both?
- You have the right to be who you really are regardless of stereotypical wishes dictated by society

Chapter 13
People Aren't Broken

They make the best choices available to them.

For me, watching TV involves a careful process of program selection. I grew up in a household where the TV was on and loud 24/7, or so it seemed. Now, the constant barrage of TV noise is unsettling. Yes, some need TV as background noise or 'company' and don't even seem to be aware it's on. Not turning the TV off when visitors arrive has always struck me as rather rude, especially when I am that visitor. However, one day my friend's habit of leaving her TV on turned out to be a bonus. That was the day I heard Dr Phil say "People aren't broken!"

Maybe I'd heard those words before, but now I was listening. Even though my body sat in my friend's lounge room, my mind had gone walkabout. It was visiting past scenarios where the truth of these words jumped out at me. All of a sudden, so much made sense.

We do everything for a reason

People aren't broken. We all do what we do because of the benefit that gives us. Even though that benefit may not seem like a benefit to others, it doesn't matter.

To illustrate this, let's revisit Dr Masaru Emoto's research on water. After reading the results of his astonishing experiments, one family decided to conduct their own experiment. They put rice in two glass jars and every day for a month said "Thank you" to one jar and "You fool" to the other. After one month, the "Thank you" rice had a mellow smell and had started to ferment. The "You fool" rice had rotted and turned black. Dr Masaru Emoto wrote about this experiment in his book and hundreds of families throughout

Japan tried this same experiment, and realised the same results. One family did something different: they added a third jar of rice then completely ignored it. What do you think happened?

The rice that was ignored actually rotted first. Even before the rice exposed to the words 'You fool'. Many others tried this intriguing variation and got the same result.

Angry attention is better than no attention

It seems that being ridiculed is not as bad as being ignored. Interesting. Dr Masaru Emoto states the most damaging form of behaviour is withholding your attention. He believes we must give children our attention and talk with them. He further believes speaking words of kindness and love should begin from the time of conception. This simply makes good sense, don't you agree?

As a young girl, I was a sulker. If I couldn't get my own way, and I rarely did, my only recourse was to sulk. Even though it didn't seem to affect my parents greatly, much to my dismay, the sulking continued.

In the light of these experiments with rice, perhaps sulking was an effective weapon. I do remember my father kneeling down before me one day, when I'd sulked for quite some time, telling me how special I was to my mother. Quite frankly, due to what I'd felt was unfair and unloving behaviour from my mother (typical teenager), I couldn't believe my father's words. However, I never forgot them. Decades later I discovered my father was not my biological father. My mother was just 18 years old when she gave birth to me, an illegitimate child. Although she was urged to give me up for adoption, she decided to keep her baby daughter. I'm glad she did.

People do what they do because it gets the result they want

Consider this: last year I trained 'Time Management' to a room of stressed out women working in the mental health field. Grants were very important to the survival of this particular organisation. Getting those grants submitted within the laid down timeframe caused much of that stress. Mandy, a mature-aged worker struggled with managing her time. She shared an example of why her to-do list rarely got done. Mandy had let one of her many bosses, Kate, know she couldn't do her grant proposal right now because others had submitted their grant proposals first. In effect Mandy was saying no, I can't do yours right now, but I will do it when it is rightfully your turn.

This was not good enough for Kate. Kate shouted, threw her arms about and just stood there. She just stood there, towering over Mandy, and would not move until Mandy agreed to do her grant proposal. Right now!

You can teach people to treat you well – or badly

Did this work? Of course it did. Mandy felt totally intimidated and agreed to work on Kate's proposal. Right now! What Mandy had just done was teach Kate how to get her own way next time too. So Kate's future strategy will be to shout, wave her arms about and stand over Mandy and she'll get her proposal done first. We train people how to treat us. Mandy had just shown Kate how to treat her like a doormat. I worked with Mandy to develop a better way to handle this next time. Because there will most definitely be a next time.

Is Kate broken or is she doing what gets her the result she needs? Kate is getting the results she needs, but at a high cost in terms of stress for all concerned. Kate's behaviour confirms she doesn't have the level of sophisticated skills needed to get organised and communicate effectively. So she resorts to bullying to get her way. Those who've experienced bullying know it's a form of cruelty. Seneca has a strong view about cruelty. *"All cruelty springs from weakness."* 4BC – AD65

Misery loves company

I'm sure you've heard the expression "Misery loves company." Walk up any city street and you'll not see many smiling faces. If people are smiling, it's because they're looking down at a message or video on their smart phone. This reminds me of a teacher who needed to address a student's lack of attention. Much to his surprise, she told him to stop reading his phone messages. She said she knew he was reading his messages because it was not normal to look down at one's crotch and smile.

But back to 'misery loves company'. Why would anyone choose to be miserable? For the same reason we choose any other emotion, it gets the result we want. The sympathy and attention of others as they offer to help can be most gratifying. This behaviour does reach a tipping point though, where it no longer returns the desired result. Unfortunately, some are so set in their behaviour, they seem unable to adapt to the new situation. Miserable people rarely get to feel good and that rubs off on you, if you allow it. If you work in an office environment, make the following into a sign and place on your desk. 'I am not interested in participating in doom and gloom.' Do you dare? Watch what happens. Of course, this won't work if you enjoy the drama of doom and gloom.

HOW Chapter 13:
People Aren't Broken – Three Rays of Light

1. People aren't broken and neither are you. We all make the best choices available to us at the time.
2. Identify one thing you do that is viewed by others as difficult behaviour, yet gets the result you want
3. What's the benefit of acting out this behaviour?

Identify Your Ray of Light: take a moment to write down what you got from this chapter:

Summary

- People aren't broken; they make the best choices available to them.
- Our words have power – as evidenced by the rice experiment.
- Some find even angry attention better than no attention.
- Give people your attention.
- We train people how to treat us.
- Being a misery can be a form of attention seeking.

Chapter 14

The Curse Of Your Comfort Zone

How was your day today?

Was it more of the same old, same old or did you do something different? You may be like many who say they're very happy with their life the way it is, thank you. These people often say things like "Been going to the same place to have my cup of coffee for years now. Why would I change? They make it exactly how I like it." They tend to be very logical "I always drive exactly the same way to work or to see my friends. Why would I choose a different, longer route? That just doesn't make sense." And of course, they're right.

It feels very comfortable to do what you've always done, even if you're not getting the results you'd prefer. We have a saying for that. "Better the devil you know than the devil you don't." And we nod our head in agreement at these wise words. They're perfectly true aren't they? I believe the only thing these words are perfectly true for is keeping you in your comfort zone, no matter how unhappy or bored or stifled you feel.

Life in the zone

Here's another common saying to guide us on our way through life "Life begins at the edge of your comfort zone." What do we mean when we talk about our comfort zone? It can be your physical environment. Some older women only feel safe in their own home. That's where they watch TV, especially the news. There aren't many good news stories on TV. And if it's on the news it has to be true, terrifyingly true.

The media is not a good guide to what's actually happening

In 2000, at the time of the Olympic Games in Sydney Australia, I backpacked solo around Italy for my 50th birthday. En route to my bucket list dream destination, the Amalfi Coast, I stopped in Naples to look around. Internet cafes can be difficult to find, but my luck was in. Sitting down and turning on the computer, I was gobsmacked to find a full inbox. Frantic family and friends warned me to avoid Naples because of the riots. Avoid the riots, they emailed, it looks really bad there! I was genuinely puzzled. Here I am in the middle of 'riot-torn Naples', with no riots to be seen. The only 'mass of people' were those crammed into cafes to watch the Olympic Games.

Remember that song lyric 'Scary movie right there on my TV'? They were singing about the 6.30PM news. That song rang true because most news programs do report events in a sensationalist, scary way. Heck, nowadays we can just sit back and enjoy real wars streamed live into our lounge rooms. Death. Famine. Pain. Danger. The world is a scary place, especially if you only experience it from within the confines of your lounge room.

You may be wondering why this chapter is called 'The Curse of Your Comfort Zone'. Operating in your comfort zone doesn't seem like such a bad thing. You do what you've always done, which results in always getting great coffee and getting to your friend's place on time. What's bad about that?

You'll never know what you never know

What if there was a place serving even better coffee and the world's best chocolate cake? You'll never discover that place because you'd rather stay with the devil you know. So the saying, 'Better the devil you know than the devil you don't' keeps us in the same old situation. We choose something we know over the unknown. When we continue to live out our lives this way, mediocrity and boredom set in.

That devilish saying is used many times in conversation and keeps people from being courageous. It's used as a cop-out, as an excuse to stay safe, to not dare to try something different.

And it's not even about staying safe sometimes. How many women have you heard complain about the way their partner treats them? Some talk of being physically or emotionally hurt, yet they still stay. These situations are complex, but often you'll hear these women say, 'Better the devil you know than the devil you don't.'

Have you noticed this saying only offers us two choices, and both choices involve devils? Where are the angels in all this?

We're all on automatic

About twenty years ago, I attended my first two-week Neuro Linguistic Programming (NLP) certification course. Of the many course activities, one sticks in my mind. To start each day, every participant had to share one thing they'd done the previous evening. The tough bit was it had to be something we'd never done before. As we were at the course for eight hours each day, this was a challenge. Most people struggled, as did I. You've picked the takeaway though haven't you? We operate on automatic. This challenge forced us to see how very much on automatic we were. Sure, some things have to be on automatic: that's a given for our survival. It didn't take long to discover how set in our ways, how deep in a rut, our lives were. (Definition of a rut: a coffin with the ends knocked out.) We all went to the same cafe for our coffee, and we always took the same route home. This is okay if you are happy with that rut, that same way of doing things. Walk around any city or suburb and tell me how many smiling faces you see? Yet we have a roof over our heads, clothes on our back and food in our fridge. Even so, the smiles are hard to find.

I've got it all but I'm still not happy

Some women have shared they feel guilty because they have everything they could want in life, but they're still not happy. I tell them they're delusional. If you truly have everything you want in your life, how could you not be happy? What's missing?

If you decide you don't deserve happiness, you're right. Life works that way. We will never find out what's missing if we stay in our comfort zone until the day we die. Remember, no one's getting out alive, so when is the right time to make the best of the rest of your life?

Let's revisit the truism 'Life begins at the edge of your comfort zone.' I cannot tell you how exhilarating it is to step out, to jump off that edge. But it sure takes guts to do that. Why is it we won't make changes to our lives until the situation gets so painful, so unbearable, that we're forced to take action? And I'm just like most others when it comes to putting up with living in the zone. My work situation had become untenable. Even though I had the security of a reasonably well-paid senior trainer position and a maintained company car, I was unhappy. Anyone who's worked in an office has experienced the politics and games played for amusement and attention. The grim faces of many team members hinted at their deep levels of dissatisfaction too. My comfort zone was far from comfortable. But it was doubtful a new employer would view a woman of 58 years favourably. Surely life had more to offer? Bravely, some said foolishly, I set out to start my own training business.

Perfect timing? Doesn't exist!

My timing in life has often been awkward. A trend continued when starting my training business in 2008, about the time the Global Financial Crisis hit. Yes, timing is everything. Australians boast the downturn missed our country. That wasn't my experience as a small business owner, especially when in the business of training. Training is always the first thing to go in any economic downturn. Which doesn't make sense, because that's when people need help on how to get through the scary mess. Somehow, I survived.

Jumping off the edge, again

This year, I've stepped out again. One of my clients is an international training company. For many years, it was good to wake up and find training gigs in my inbox. What wasn't so good was being paid the wholesale fee. Fair enough though, all I had to do was deliver the training. And initially, I didn't want to bother with those cold calls and deal with the rejection. There was a further price to pay: time.

Good client feedback resulted in heavily scheduled months. Often up to 14 training days each month. Add one or two days of travel for each gig and there was little free time in the month. It looked glamorous though, flying all around Australia and New Zealand. But this quickly wore off. The exhausting schedules took their toll. As already shared, I was unhappy.

Stepping outside my comfort zone this time was really scary. They were my biggest client so how crazy was I to terminate our agreement? But I was exhausted, stressed and over it. So terminate I did. Still scared I was, but alive I am. Here's another saying 'One door closes and another door opens.' The interesting thing is, that door was always there. I just couldn't see it before. Like magic, many other doors are opening. For the first time in six years, I'm getting calls off my website. New ideas keep popping into my mind, perhaps because I'm not so tired now. Life is good.

Your life in the comfort zone

So here's the takeaway. Jump!

You'll never discover your potential if you stay tightly curled up like a bud. You'll never discover the flower you really are if you don't allow yourself to blossom. Never! Now is the time to realise your desire. In Chapter 10, you read the five regrets people had on their deathbeds. Did you pick up the

Live before you die.

main theme? People regretted what they had NOT done, not what they'd done. Don't *you* go to your grave regretting what you didn't do. Life is an adventure. Take some risks. Live.

And finally *"In any given moment we have two options: to step forward into growth or to step back into safety."* – Abraham Maslow

HOW Chapter 14:
The Curse of Your Comfort Zone –
Three Rays of Light

1. Do you ever complain about the same old, same old? If you do, try this: every day for the next ten days you must do one thing differently to how you've always done it. This could be going to a different cafe or driving home a different way. But the catch is, for each of the following days you must do other different things. They can't be the same different things from previous days. You may be surprised at what you discover.

2. Why is 'the devil we know better than the devil we don't'? How easily we use such sayings. These words automatically roll off your tongue, but what do they really mean? Catch yourself saying them then challenge the concept behind these words. Women living in abusive situations use this as an acceptable reason to stay.

3. If my children remember only one thing from my motherly teachings, I hope it's this: "It's good to plan, so do that. Always remember this: when you take that first step you will see things it was not possible to see before. Then your plan may change, that's okay. Keep taking those steps and expect revelations." Just take that first step out of your comfort zone and your life will never be the same again.

Identify Your Ray of Light: take a moment to write down what you got from this chapter:

_____

_____

Summary

- Be wary of the comfort zone.
- You might feel comfortable doing all the things you're familiar with, but it's very limiting and ultimately unfulfilling.
- 'Comfortable' is another word for 'not open to anything new'.
- The world around us can be quite different to that presented by the media.
- It's never too late to do something new, even on your deathbed, but why wait until then?
- It's a cliché, but it's true – as one door closes another opens.

Chapter 15
Why We Don't Speak Our Truth

Why don't we speak our truth? What is it that stops us from telling others how we truly feel about what they just did or said? I've asked these questions time and time again during my workshops. There are many answers; what would your answer be?

Believe it or not, the main reason given is "I don't want to hurt their feelings." If you're anything like those 12,500 workshop participants, that probably was your answer too. So, if your true intent is 'to not hurt their feelings' surely you'd have to ask them what would hurt their feelings? It could sound like this "What is it I could do or say that would hurt your feelings?" Not one person has ever admitted to asking that question or any type of discovery question.

Not one person has ever asked

Think about that. Not one person out of 12,500 has ever taken the time to ask the other person what would hurt their feelings.

So we don't truly know what would hurt their feelings, but we sure do know what hurt ours. So we treat others as if they are just like us. If it hurts our feelings, surely it hurts theirs too? Or, if it doesn't hurt our feelings why are they acting so offended? Not a good strategy Sherlock.

Have you noticed people are different? I'm sure you've noticed not everyone has your uncommon good sense. We all know others are not like us, yet here we go again, treating them as if they are just like us, when they're not.

The perfect question

A manager shared the story of an unusual question his new team member asked at their very first meeting. She said to him, "What is it I could do or say that would put your nose out of joint?" No one had ever asked a question like that before, so he wasn't sure how to answer. Thinking quickly, he came up with a short list of just one thing.

What a clever question to ask, don't you think? This woman laid her cards on the table straight away. Now she had a valuable piece of information she could use if and when a situation called for it. As for the manager, it certainly caused him to ponder on what does get up his nose. Asking this one question resulted in clearer communication all around.

Isn't this another perspective to WIIFM (What's In It For Me)? Here's how WIIFM applies to the concept in this chapter; we don't speak our truth because we don't want to hurt other's feelings. Yes, but why don't we want to hurt their feelings? Is it because, if we hurt their feelings then they might not like us?

Baby boomers seek approval

Have you ever noticed this? Yes, this is a generalisation about baby boomers, but it certainly rings true for me at times. We can feel quite disconcerted if we sense others disapprove of what we've just said or done. For example, have you ever been told you have a certain 'look'? Others pick this up, notably your children, which is challenging because you've never seen this so-called 'look'. So now we get hurt and, even as an adult, can act in a sulky way. Not me though, finally got rid of that behaviour.

There's another major reason why many people find it difficult to speak their truth. Did your mum ever say to you "If you can't say anything nice, then don't say anything at all"?

If you say this, please stop right now

Why am I suggesting you stop saying this? As more and more disclosures surface of the abuse little children have suffered, the real and present danger of this expression becomes clear. Things that are not nice happen to little children. Things that are not nice happen to big children. Yes, things that are not nice happen to us as well, but as adults, we have more power over the situation. As adults we know about options open to us, even if we don't take advantage of them. Whether you believe this or not, if that saying is playing in the background of your mind, if it pops up every now and again, it impacts your current actions.

And surely you'd have to ask yourself what is meant by the word 'nice'. Let's face it, saying something is 'nice' is a lacklustre compliment. Apart from highlighting a serious deficiency in one's vocabulary, it also sounds suspiciously like a backhanded compliment. Notice how many times, and in what circumstances, you use the word 'nice'.

At first, participants in my seminars push back when they're asked to stop saying this phrase. However, upon hearing the explanation many are horrified because not only have they said it to their children, they are now using this expression with their grandchildren.

One woman shared this story to show how easily young children can misinterpret adult words. Sitting with her brother in the lounge room, a little girl was excited to be watching her first ever TV show. The show ended with the cowboys hanging all the Indians from a tree. The little girl was distraught and could only be pacified when her mother said, "Don't worry darling, it's just a game. When the cameras stop filming, all those Indians get up and walk away. This made the little girl happy and she raced outside to play a game with her brother. To this day, her mother doesn't know what made her go outside to check on her children, but she was so glad she did. The mother found her daughter hanging from the tree, her face turning blue as the rope tightened around her neck. Happily playing the part of the cowboy, the brother pulled the rope tighter.

You've probably guessed the woman telling this story was that same little girl hanging from the tree. Now standing before us, she asked everyone to realise how trusting and literal children will be with your words.

Consider then their interpretation of this saying "Little children should be seen and not heard." Danger! Danger! Danger!

Fear of the consequences

Another reason we don't speak our truth is fear of the consequences.

Recently, a public servant shared the acronym CARE 'Cover Arse Retain Employment'. Due to my extensive experience across all industries, I well know this acronym does not only apply to the public service sector.

We laugh at the line "Does my bum look big in this?" Seriously though, how is one supposed to respond to this? This is known as an entrapment question. You're damned if you say 'yes' and you're damned if you say 'no'. The woman asking this question suspects her bum does look big in it, so she won't believe you when you say "No!" The sage male response to this question is "If you're going to ask me expect a truthful answer or don't ask me." Trends blossom and change the acceptable landscape of our body. These days, women with big bums smile smugly as the 'big bum' trend bites women with small bums.

Another trend, a disturbing one, is using political correctness as an excuse to shut people down from speaking their truth. Here's a twist: some don't speak their truth to ensure another suffers. In the workplace, this is known as 'malicious compliance'. Let's say your new boss wants to implement a new practice. However, her idea is not new. Your previous boss had the same idea last year. It was a disaster. Because you've taken a dislike to the new boss, you don't tell her. Watching the expected disaster unfold, you feel safe from accusations of wrongdoing. After all, you were only doing as directed. Not true! Malicious compliance is the behaviour of a person who intentionally inflicts harm by strictly following the orders of management.

Verbalise don't Internalise

Tough love lesson of not speaking your truth

If you continue to 'shut up and put up' there is a price to pay. Every time you don't express your version of the truth you will suffer a far greater consequence. As a woman over 60, the consequences of 'holding your tongue' may be showing up in your life right now. The internal rage at the injustices suffered, the humiliation put up with, the dreams long lost must eventually show, in some way. When we internalise instead of verbalising, our body keeps score. It's not an airy-fairy statement that stress kills; extensive scientific research now confirms this. Thinking so much, but saying so little for so long is a destructive process. When will it be okay to have the right to say how things are for you, to speak your truth?

This chapter presents clear reasons why women don't speak their truth. Your real reasons for not speaking your truth are known only to you. Are those reasons still valid? Is it time to start speaking your truth?

HOW Chapter 15: Why We Don't Speak Our Truth – Three Rays of Light

1. The beginning of this chapter asked why you don't speak your truth; what was your answer?
2. Verbalise don't internalise. Sounds sensible right? But how do you do that, after so many years of internalising? Sadly, when 'stuff' eventually spills out, it does so in an inappropriate and aggressive way. Naturally, the response you'll get will be a defensive one. As tempers flare, the ability to communicate real feelings disappears.
3. Sickness and disease are an inevitable outcome of holding so much inside. Resorting to temporary solutions, such as 'mother's little helper' (nickname for valium), does little to reduce inside pain and torment. What to do? Become aware of what needs to change, decide to change then take action to change. But first, you need to acknowledge you're worth that effort. You must decide you deserve better ... because you do.

Identify Your Ray of Light: take a moment to write down what you got from this chapter:

_____

_____

Summary

- Speak your truth, even if you think you'll hurt the feelings of others.
- What is true for you isn't necessarily true for others.
- The words we say to children, and that we hear as children, resonate further and deeper than we think.
- A reason we don't speak our truth is fear of consequences.
- There will be a price to pay if you continue to 'shut up'.
- When we internalise, the body reacts.

Chapter 16

Meet Your Survival Strategy; Change Your Life

"Holding onto anger is like drinking poison and expecting the other person to die." – Buddha

Do you know what you look like when you're angry?

You certainly know how you feel, but I bet you have no clue how you look.

But before we consider that, let's look at the question 'Why do we get angry?'

Why do we get angry?

Thousands of people have answered this question and certainly offered interesting answers. Common ones are: they shouldn't do that, it was my turn, she took too long to deliver my order, he laughed at me, they wouldn't do what I asked, he's stupid, they shouldn't show this stuff on TV. And she cut in front of me, it doesn't look good, I'm too fat, no one likes me, I hate my hair, this coffee is cold, they're naughty and so the long list goes on, and on.

I've challenged these answers by asking why do we get angry. At the tippy-top of all these responses, there's really only one reason we do get angry. What is that one reason?

We don't like not getting our own way

Finally, someone will say it. The reason we get angry is because we are not getting our own way. Yes, the world is not dancing to our tune. Like the big kids we still are deep down, our bottom lip juts out. With total certainty, we know our version of how life should be is the right way. We wouldn't believe something if it wasn't the right way. Sound familiar?

You may not agree with the idea that we get angry because we don't get our own way. I can understand that because it does sound rather selfish and egotistical. After all, who are we to demand the world acts according to our rules and regulations? But we do. Next time you get angry, whether you show it or not, stop and dig deep for the real reason you're angry. Okay, there might be a .5 per cent chance it's because of some other reason. If you do discover that other reason, please let me know. Always open to new learning.

Anger is all about me

So far, in my experience across thousands of participants, when people take the time to reflect on why they truly get angry, it becomes obvious. This reflection is important because when we get angry, we do nasty things to ourselves. Apart from looking scary, intimidating and most unattractive, we are hurting our own bodies. Being angry, or any other fearful emotion, causes damaging reactions in our bodily systems. Sure, pat yourself on the back for going to the gym, or running, or any other exercise. But all that good work will not be effective if you are inclined to be constantly angry. What exercise does, if you allow it, is to give you space to think. By think, I don't mean 'I said, she said' thoughts; that's just stewing and brewing. Next time you're feeling angry, go for a quick walk. Notice I didn't say go for a power walk (although you could). A quick walk with some swinging of your arms is sufficient. Even if you are determined to stay angry (because you're right and they're wrong), it will not be possible to stay angry at the same high level. Your body will naturally release endorphins so, even if it's against your will, you will start to feel better. I know. It can be annoying to feel better when you want to stay angry.

Even if the word 'exercise' makes you want to vomit, get up, get out and get walking. Before long, you will feel more alive, alert and yes, even happier.

Do you get angry when people are late?

I always got angry if people turned up late for our meeting. As a proud on-time fanatic, I felt disrespected when others didn't value me enough to be on time. This stemmed from my first position as a personal assistant. My boss was never on time for her meetings. Clients often became annoyed and blamed me for her tardiness. She told me her time was far too valuable to be waiting on others to turn up. Therefore, her simple remedy was to arrive late. And as she was paying for my time, waiting was part of my duty statement. Somehow, that explanation never felt right.

Many years later, I discovered NLP, which offered a valid explanation for why people are late. According to NLP, people relate to the concept of time in two ways. Basically, one type live 'in time' meaning they're caught up in the moment and easily lose track of schedules. They struggle to break away from conversations to keep appointments, often because they are so engrossed in the content. The other type live 'through time' meaning they keep track of their schedule, easily cutting a conversation short to honour a time commitment. Recognising my type as 'through time' and understanding not everyone was like me, I grew more tolerant of those who were late. If this quick description of these time types intrigues you, any good book on NLP will open up a tool box of goodies to explore. With my new understanding, I rarely became angry when people were late.

Getting angry is stressful and, as we know, numerous scientific studies have proven stress kills. Additionally, many studies identify strong, negative emotions as a leading cause of disease, including cancer. Bitterness, resentment, unhappiness and other emotional reactions are aggravated by our perception of life's situations.

Isn't anger good?

Doesn't anger get that emotional turmoil out and clear the air? Yes, hurling hurtful words can clear the air, and the house, and the workplace. You are the only one left to assess the damage done.

Words have power. Did you grow up with this saying "Sticks and stones may break my bones but names will never hurt me"? We all know that's not true. As already shared, I cannot remember one broken bone from my childhood, but easily remember the taunts and nicknames endured. Angry words are damaging. It does no good to say "I didn't mean it." That's like taking one of your best dinner plates outside and throwing it on the ground. Now say to the broken plate "I'm sorry." Did the plate come back together again? Even if you lovingly glue the pieces back together, the integral strength of the plate will never be as it was before.

To illustrate how actions affect relationships, a teacher conducted an insightful experiment. Her students were told to scrunch a sheet of paper into a tight ball. Then they were directed to drop their ball on the ground and jump up and down on it. Finally, the students were told to pick up their flattened paper blobs and smooth them out. No matter how hard they tried, the paper could not be made smooth. It remained crumpled and dirty. After such damaging treatment, the sheet of paper will never, ever be the same again.

If you consider feeling angry is a sign that something needs to be looked at, then anger can be useful. But anger is not useful if it is used as a weapon against yourself and others. Remember, 'anger' is just one letter away from 'danger'.

"*Speak when you are angry and you will make the best speech you'll ever regret.*" – Ambrose Bierce

When we get angry the red mist descends and the heat rises. We can't think, hear or see very well. That's a sure sign your survival strategy has kicked in.

Your survival strategy

Psychologists tell us our survival strategy is in place by the time we're three years old. This makes sense. As a cave baby, you would not become a cave toddler if you didn't develop excellent survival strategies. And it's certainly true our DNA hasn't changed much over the last 10,000 years, but our environment sure has. So your survival strategy is what you instinctively do when you feel threatened. But take note, it's what you instinctively do based on the circumstances of your life when you were just three years old.

This means we instinctively respond to threats, whether real or imagined, as if we are still three years old. Even as adults, haven't we caught ourselves reacting to a situation in a childish manner? Surely I'm not the only one who confesses to doing just that.

Understand what your survival strategy is – only then can you change it

My experience shows many people are not aware of their survival strategy. If you're not aware of it, you can't change it. What causes you to feel threatened varies greatly and depends on your upbringing and culture. For example, two Filipina women shared they felt threatened when a voice was raised at them. We're not talking shouting: simply talking a little bit louder caused these women to feel threatened.

You may remember my description of 'getting angry'. When the red mist descends and the heat rises, you experience powerful emotions. You'll have your own potent words describing what it means to 'get angry'. Whatever those words are, they powerfully impact your body, your mind and alter your perception of reality. One way to shortcut this envelopment of red mist and flames is to have an understanding of our survival strategy.

Our automatic survival strategy takes many forms. Visual clues include rising up to make ourselves appear bigger, shrinking down so we're less of a target, gritting teeth, thinning lips, clenching fists, squinting eyes, looking down our noses, grimacing, avoiding eye contact or glaring. Sometimes our voice tone will be lower, we may talk much slower or our tone rises to a squealing pitch and we talk very quickly.

The point is your survival strategy kicks in automatically and invisibly ... to you. You will not be aware how you present and the threat you now pose to others. But who is aware? Yes, everyone else in your life. How can you find out what your survival strategy is? Ask! Ask someone you can rely on to tell you the truth of their senses.

This is important

Here's why this is important to discover. Let's say you work in a store in customer service. Looking up as a customer approaches, you sigh and think, "Here comes another one." Instinctively, you brace for the onslaught from another unhappy customer. What if your survival strategy involves making yourself bigger? What if you slit your eyes and clench your teeth? What if you thin your lips (which means you're certainly not smiling)? Picture how you look to the customer. The customer is expecting a fight anyway. He now thinks "I knew it! These 'No questions asked' returns are always a lie." So the customer instantly, and without even being aware of it, reacts to your body language. "Yes" he thinks "looks like I'm not getting my money back." So your customer automatically launches into his survival strategy. Two people posturing in their survival strategy are like two matches bursting into flame. And that starts the escalation into conflict.

Now you are aware of survival strategies, look for them in other people. Recognise them for what they are and you will not get so upset over their childish responses. This knowledge will help you have more control over your responses. Understanding survival strategies is an extremely useful conflict resolution tool.

A case study

One night, as I was getting ready to go out, my lawyer friend waited in the lounge room. Suddenly, the sound of smashing glass echoed through the hallway. Racing out, my worst fear was confirmed when I saw my favourite handed-down-from-generation-to-generation vase smashed into little pieces on the floor. My friend was very tall, yet here he was hunched down like a child with his hands over his eyes. Although his carelessness made me angry, his childlike posture stopped me from venting. How could I get upset at this child before me? To this day, I have no clue whether his actions were his survival strategy or whether he was being a very, very clever lawyer.

In my work, I meet all kinds of people who are struggling with the demands of everyday life. Some people declare they like living on the edge. They seriously believe if you're not living on the edge, you're taking up too much space! I prefer to take a step back. Heights scare me.

We all have free will. We all have the right to live our lives as we choose. Therefore, it naturally follows we must accept the consequences of those choices. If you don't like how your life is unfolding, do something different. Take responsibility for the results you're getting now. The word 'responsibility' means you have the ability to respond. Everyone has that ability. Don't let anyone take that from you. Know it's your response to what happens that creates your reality. Period.

Make it your mission to discover your survival strategy, because when you can control your automatic response to given situations, your life will truly change.

<u>HOW</u> Chapter 16:
Meet Your Survival Strategy;
Change Your Life – Three Rays of Life

1. What did you identity as the one reason that makes you angry? Did you agree with the explanation that we get angry because we don't get our own way? If not, why not?

2. Please set out to discover your survival strategy. The first step is to write down how you think you look when you get angry. Write it all down. What happens to your lips, your jaw, your eyes, your teeth and your hands? Notice all the things others would see that shows you are angry. This includes how your voice sounds, the volume of your words and how you hold your body. Write down everything. Secondly, ask someone to tell you how you look when you are angry. If you give them the right to be honest, you may well be amazed at their answer. How does it compare to your written down observations?

3. Identity three situations that make you angry. Delve deep into why they make you angry. What are the triggers that cause that emotion to erupt? As you read in this chapter, my angry response to people running late for an agreed time stemmed from the egotistical attitude of my boss.

Identify Your Ray of Light: take a moment to write down what you got from this chapter:

_____

_____

Summary

- We get angry ... because we don't get our own way.
- It's time to grow up.
- Anger impacts on our body.
- Do you live 'in time' or 'through time'?
- Words have power and not all of it is good.
- Actions affect relationships.
- Anger is not useful if it is used as a weapon against yourself and others.
- Your survival strategy is usually based on circumstances you faced in your early childhood.
- If you don't like how your life is unfolding, do something different.
- Learn your survival strategy, because when you can control your automatic response, your life will truly change.

Chapter 17
The Word Hidden In Belief

"The roots of discontent are internal, and each person must untangle them with his or her own power." – Mihalyi Csikszentmihalyi author of *Flow*

You've read the books; you've attended the seminars, but nothing has worked. As one woman sadly shared with her group, "My life still sucks." Do personal development seminars really work?

You be the judge of my story

Three decades ago, I was very excited to be attending my very first personal development seminar. Although I'd paid a high price to be walking through the doors of the Entertainment Centre in Perth, I was excited. I was excited because my life sucked, and these guys had promised attendance would change my life. The only speaker I still remember is Jim Rohn. As Jim walked onto the stage, I leant forward because this was it! Secrets were about to be revealed, and I was here to hear them. Pen poised, heart pounding ... I was ready. Bring it on!

I remember walking back out those same doors feeling totally disgusted and angry. "What a rip-off!" my mind screamed. The big secret was the seminar title: 'Change your mind; Change your life.' What utter rubbish! It's not about me; it's about them! It's about the world and how unfair it is. It's about those people in my life who are selfish and mean. IT'S NOT ABOUT ME! I'm a good person who deserves better ...

It really is all about you

Reading these words again, I cannot help but wonder how different my life would've been if I'd got that 'secret' way back then. But it was another decade before the truth of *Change your mind; Change your life* slowly dawned and revealed its life-changing power.

My personal development journey has often been painful and slow, but as I sit here typing these words, I am grateful beyond words. How many books have I read? I never kept count, but countless many have rested in my hands. How many seminars have I attended? I'd need more than my fingers and toes to count them. Do personal development seminars and books work? You wouldn't still be reading this book if you didn't think so.

Yes, personal development seminars and books work. BUT, and as you can see, it's a big 'but', only if YOU TAKE ACTION, if *you do* something with that new idea. Even if you only take one thing away and make one change in your life, your time sitting in that seminar has been well spent. As you know, I've been a trainer for 31 years now. Do I think I know it all? Absolutely not! Participants often hear me declare "I'm a work in progress." Every group teaches me at least one new thing. The day I say I know it all is the day my ability to be an engaging and effective trainer is gone– forever. Due to an intense curiosity about life and how we create it, I'm always looking for new ways to offer useful strategies. My clients know I'm not a 'tick-in-the-box' trainer. This means some of the topic content can be confronting, because it causes people to examine why they do what they do. Stepping outside their comfort zone is necessary, because only then do they see the very real possibility of living a better life.

Why do we do what we do?

Now that is the million dollar question. Like always, there is never just one answer, so let's look at one major factor that causes us to do what we do.

First though, can you recall a time you said something and wondered afterwards where those words came from? I clearly recall one day, as a young mum with two young children, telling my daughter off. Can't remember what she did, but I do remember shouting angrily at her. Bending over to drive my point home, my face not far from hers, something happened. It was as if the scene was frozen as these words exploded in my head "What are you saying? It doesn't make sense!"

Shocked, the awful truth hit me

Those words I shouted that day, they were not my words. The fog lifted as the image of my mother's face materialised. Her face was close to mine as she bent down, shouting those very same words. As a little girl, the meaning of her words never made sense. But mother's mood was made clear by the tone of her voice and her angry look. Now, here I was, repeating the same pattern of behaviour. Know what was really weird? As an adult, I still didn't understand the words coming out of my own mouth. Yet, here I was acting like a robot and shouting them at my little girl. Right there and then, I swore never to do that again, and I never did. My belief is that when you decide to do something, truly decide, then you are unstoppable.

Is that really true?

If that were true, why is it so many fail with their decision to stop smoking, or drinking, or eating chocolate? (Actually, forget about stopping eating chocolate; that's never going to happen.) I believe it's because they don't truly decide to stop. Even though they declare so to the outside world, it's not the truth of their internal world. Remember, people aren't broken. We need to look at why we're smoking, drinking or eating chocolate (and we all know there are other 'Should Stop Doing Habits'). The major reason we do what we do is because we get a benefit from doing it. When we uncover that benefit, we must then look at the consequences of our choice. How can we compare why we do something (the beneficial consequences) to why we shouldn't do something (the harmful consequences)? One way is to imagine holding the beneficial consequences in the palm of one hand and the harmful consequences in the palm of the other. Doing this helps us see the whole picture. Simply choose one. You can't have both. Once you've make that decision, know you've made that decision with volition. Yes, I know this sounds too easy. Give it a go anyway. Don't complain about your hangover or the fact your favourite dress no longer fits if you're not prepared to do something about it.

Why is it that so many people attend personal development seminars on how to get rich, or how to find a soul mate, how to succeed in a business, how to be happy, yet never succeed in achieving any of these desires? That's why we're here, to hear our own thinking as we read this chapter on beliefs.

Beliefs: that which we hold dear

According to the Encyclopaedia Britannica, beliefs are a mental attitude of acceptance or assent toward a proposition without the full intellectual knowledge required to guarantee its truth.

Phew, now we've got that over and done with, let's look at the impact of our beliefs on the results we get today. Beliefs are your mindset and determine your course through life. So let's look around at your life, at what you have your mind set on. If you lack confidence, courage, celebration, money, friends, health, happiness or any other 'lack' then it's probably because of a belief you have around that. You may dispute the addition of health as a result of your beliefs. "What about inherited diseases?" you protest "I can't be blamed for them!" This isn't about blame. This is about discovery. The scary thing is most of us have no clue about what we truly believe.

Let's start at the beginning

Psychologists tell us the age from zero to seven years old is known as the 'imprint period'. This is the period when we soak up all the information needed to survive in our world. The main providers of this information are the big people in our lives; parents, older siblings, aunties and uncles, etc. This information is vital to our survival and locks in patterns of behaviour. The trouble is, we are not aware of what that automatic, locked in behaviour is. If we are not aware of our automatic behaviour, we cannot ask, "Does that behaviour still serve me?"

Here's an example. Here you are, six years old and about to cross the road (in Australia). A parent is holding your hand and directs you to look to the right, look to the left and look to the right again. This is important training, as it increases the likelihood you'll cross the road safely. You're grown up now and on holiday ... in America. You're about to cross the road. Which way do you look first? Logically, you'd look to the left, but many times, that's not what happens. Australians have been brought up to look to the right first. It's ingrained behaviour and we don't even think about it, not even in a foreign country. So, without thinking we step out and look the wrong way. Many session participants have shared their close call, their brush with death.

Are you on auto?

So I ask you, what is it you are doing right now that's on automatic? What is it you are doing that worked for you as a child, but isn't working for you as an adult? Unless you dive deep and examine your behaviour, you will never know. Discovering this on your deathbed is too late. Let's look at it now. Automatic behaviour is based on that which you believe is true.

How do we develop these beliefs we hold so dear? As already discussed, our parents, family and friends play a big part in shaping what we hold as true. The rules of society, our culture and our gender influence our thoughts and impact our lives. Family dynamics contribute greatly to how we view life. I know I'm not the only baby boomer whose decision to support a particular political party was based solely on my father's preference. Strong emotional events fashion our perspectives and cement our beliefs on how life is.

Here's the point. Have you ever been wrong? Have you ever been proven wrong on a dearly held belief? A belief you've held as true all your life, and now you find to be untrue. Now your beliefs don't match up to reality ... how does that feel? It feels extremely uncomfortable and is often referred to as cognitive dissonance.

In psychology, cognitive dissonance is the excessive mental stress and discomfort experienced by an individual who holds two or more contradictory beliefs, ideas, or values at the same time.

The real damage of cognitive dissonance

"Sometimes people hold a core belief that is very strong. When they are presented with evidence that works against that belief, the new evidence cannot be accepted. It would create a feeling that is extremely uncomfortable called cognitive dissonance. And because it is so important to protect the core belief, they will rationalise, ignore and even deny anything that doesn't fit in with the core belief." – Franz Fanon

The tragic story of Ignaz Semmelweis perfectly illustrates the real damage of cognitive dissonance. In 1840 Semmelweis, a Hungarian physician, noticed something very puzzling about his two maternity clinics. The maternity clinic run by midwives had a much lower mortality rate than the one run by doctors. After observing each clinic's processes, he made a startling discovery. Midwives washed their hands. Semmelweis then instituted a policy of doctors washing their hands after handling dead bodies and before handling mothers and their babies. The result was a 90% drop of the mortality rate in the doctor's clinic. Unfortunately, the germ theory of disease had not yet been developed. So despite his proven results, Semmelweis's observations conflicted with established scientific and medical opinions of the time and his ideas were rejected. Additionally, some doctors were offended at the suggestion they were not clean. He was ignored, ridiculed and mocked by his peers and finally committed to a mental institution. A vast number of mothers and their babies died due to ego and an inability to accept evidence that contradicted core beliefs. One can only speculate at the torment Semmelweis endured when he witnessed so many unnecessary deaths.

New discoveries in psychology and neuroscience have further demonstrated our pre-existing beliefs can skew our thoughts and colour our most dispassionate and logical conclusions. It seems only psychotics operate in an emotional vacuum.

Are you a fan of science fiction?

I was born holding a science fiction book in my hands. Those advances in science, medicine and technology we hear about; I've known about them for a long time. Much of what was once science fiction is now science fact. Thinking about this, one woman remembered her conversation with an extremely protective father. As his daughters grew older, he lamented losing control over their whereabouts. He wished he could attach devices to the underside of their cars so he could track where they were at all times. She recalled scoffing at his words, thinking him to be fanciful. That conversation took place 40 years ago. Those devices are commonplace these days. Good news for overprotective dads but not, I suspect, for their daughters.

Readers of science fiction develop the ability to see the world, indeed our universe, in an entirely different way. Minds are stretched and opened to see unique, often weird, possibilities and how to apply them to current situations.

Eons ago, I read a science fiction story highlighting the control authority figures exert over the people ... for their own good.

After years of searching, an archaeologist discovers stone tablets from a little known ancient culture. She struggles to decipher their language, but eventually breaks the code and translates one stone tablet. Shocked at the secret now in plain view, she is unsure how to handle this explosive revelation. Knowing she cannot 'unknow' what has been revealed, she takes her translation direct to the King. The King is deeply troubled. This translation had the power to undermine the beliefs and values of his entire Kingdom. He reads the blasphemous words again. "We thanked the gods for their magic. We bowed in appreciation of their wisdom in healing the sickness that cursed our people. We worshiped them for the tools they gave us. We begged them not to leave, but leave they did. Before the last god vanished into the shining circle, he turned and said 'We are not gods. We are men, as are you. We come from another world. Do not worship us; we are not gods.' We will forever worship these gods for the goodness and blessings they gifted to our people."

The King's people worshipped these very same gods. Their lives were shaped around the beliefs and values handed down from them. The few who did not believe, who doubted the wisdom, goodness and laws of the gods were hunted down and slaughtered like the non-believers and animals they were.

For the good of the people, no doubt can ever be cast on the gods and the validity of the law of the land. Chaos and revolution would result, and many lives would be lost. And the King knew he would no longer be the ruler of his kingdom. The faith must be maintained, at any cost. Not daring to consult with his advisors, the King takes swift action. Only one person can know the truth of this translation. Within an hour, the archaeologist is dead and every single stone tablet is destroyed. Behold, the people must continue to live a lie; it is for their own good.

"In a time of deceit, telling the truth is a revolutionary act." – George Orwell

Be ready to be shocked

Discovering a long held belief is not true delivers a devastating blow to the fabric, the very foundation of one's life.

Do you know people who always need to be right? The ones who continue to argue their point, even when you've offered convincing evidence they're not? Are you that person? Linda was. During her formative years, many nights were spent lying in bed listening to her parents arguing about who was right. Therefore, she became that person who needed to be right. Indeed, her self-esteem depended on always being right.

When we always need to be right, we dig a deep pit of righteousness and stand entrenched in our perception of truth. Therefore, when we're in conversation with someone who's taking a different position to what we believe, we stop listening. We go into our head and say "That's just their BS!" (BS meaning 'Belief System' of course). We decide it's our moral duty to tell them the truth of the matter, so we disappear into our head space to develop our defence. The minute the other stops talking, we launch in with our pearls of wisdom. This is not a good strategy. Immediately, you're accused of not listening. And they're right. Listening with the intent to reply means you cannot listen. You heard their words, but you certainly didn't hear the meaning of those words.

The word hidden in belief

You can see it, can't you? Many are fascinated to find the word 'lie' hidden in belief. If another doesn't believe as we do, then we hold their belief to be a lie. A lie meaning it's not the real truth, as we know it. And we're right! How easily we lay claim to knowing the truth. How awkward we feel when we're proven wrong. That 'lie' refers to our own misguided and untrue belief.

The two most commonly held beliefs about life

If it's true that what we believe determines our results—and it is true—are there commonly held beliefs? Indeed there are. This has to be the case when we're brought up in the same culture, in the same era, with the same wars, the same global issues, the same environmental concerns, the same technology and the same biological needs.

As women over 60, we've had many years of soaking up information, of living different situations, of employing many solutions. This library of experience and knowledge is a valuable resource, yet there are times we deny this value.

Just like you, my life is rich with stories from the journey through my pre-determined road map and the many detours I've taken. Some of those detours led to vital lessons from an assortment of teachers, guides, mentors and coaches. From all these experiences, including my work with over 12,500 workshop participants, I've found people hold two common beliefs about themselves:

1. **I'm not good enough.** (I'm not enough.) How readily does this belief pop up in your mind? Going for that promotion? Ha ha ha ... who do you think you are? You won't get it so just forget even trying. So you don't. After all, rejection is painful so why put yourself through that.
   Many women have shared stories confirming how this belief stopped them from doing better with their lives. Last year,

after conducting a team building session for an aged care organisation in Northern Tasmania, a young woman told her story. This young woman was not a beauty by any standard. She had buckteeth, wore thick lenses and her face was scarred by acne. As I type these words, I see her face and feel her anguish. She said how glad she was to have attended the session. She now believed she was good enough. Her next words almost undid me. She'd realised she didn't have to believe what they've said about her all these years. As I drove to the airport with wet eyes, I could only hope she now had the courage to ignore those careless comments. My belief is we have the power to change the landscape of our life. It's not easy, but it's absolutely doable.

There are so many stories I could share with you to illustrate this point. But let's look at just one more. After a training workshop to a large government department in Queensland, my client sat down to debrief her session. Suddenly, she burst into tears. As we'd just spent six hours exploring "How to Manage Emotions', I realised I'd not done a very good job. Calming down, she shared the words her father had hurled at her when she was only seven years old. "You will never amount to anything! You will only ever be good enough to be a statue in the park and have pigeons shit on you!" It was easy to remain silent for a moment as I wondered at the devastation these words would've inflicted on the fragile self of a seven-year-old child. When such stories are shared, it fills me with great sadness to know parents can visit such pain on those they've brought into this world.

This woman's story is sad, but what's even sadder is she still believes it. Imagine how this belief has worked in the background of her life. What opportunities did she fear to take? What road did she avoid? What love did she deny? I know what you're thinking "But a parent mistreating their child often leads to the child developing the determination to rise up and prove their parent wrong." Perhaps. Either way, the fact is these children struggle to accept their parents don't love them. Often they conclude they are not good enough to earn that love.

2. **I don't belong.** The need to belong is in our DNA. As part of the survival of our species, it is important to belong to a clan, tribe or social group. With so many ways to connect online these days, how can we not feel like we belong? Although myriad social platforms provide a way to connect with literally thousands globally, we have to ask "Is this enough?" Many read posts boasting fame and fortune and feel they're missing out. Some even start to think they're not normal, not like everyone else and just not good enough. And don't think these platforms are just for kids. The largest growing demographic on Facebook is women over 50. That's why their children are deserting Facebook for other avenues of expression their parents don't know about, yet. This feeling of 'not belonging' is damaging to one's sense of well-being. Feeling one doesn't belong leads to isolation, lack of self-esteem and wondering if life is worth living.

Mary's Dilemma

Mary walked into the lunch room and saw her team gathered in the corner. She stopped when they burst into laughter. One of her team members, Anne, looked over at Mary and then quickly looked back to the group. Mary felt sick. She just knew they were laughing and talking about her. She spun around and stormed out. Later that day, Anne greeted Mary with a smile. Mary, still feeling humiliated, ignored Anne. Puzzled, Anne asked her colleague "What's the matter with Mary today?" No one could explain what the matter with Mary was. As the days went by and Mary continued to live the hurt, people reacted by excluding her from conversations. Besides, they said, she'd always been high maintenance. Anne tried to have a quiet chat with Mary to discover the reason for her behaviour. But Mary had nothing to say, especially to Anne.

Let's step back and have a look at this situation. Is it possible the girls could've been laughing at something else? Is it possible that Mary's entrance into the lunchroom was just bad timing? Are you thinking how absurd this whole scenario is and it couldn't possibly be true? Perhaps you think I made it up, and haven't done a very convincing job of it either. True story! One work group, which included Mary, shared this story. Mary agreed she had created a self-fulfilling prophecy. Whilst she was not the most popular girl in the office, she still felt she belonged. Mary's home life contributed to her lack of self-worth. She'd suffered a rocky start to her day, so instantly jumped to assuming the team were laughing at her. Mary knew it was her own response that created a situation she feared.

Think now of a time in your life when you totally misread a situation. We've all had them and, let's be honest, more than one. Remember how bad you felt when you found out the true story. But that's what we do. Based on the meaning we give a scenario, we jump to a conclusion and act accordingly. This conclusion is based on our past experiences. If we don't know the truth of the current situation, we base our conclusion (the meaning) on what happened in our past. This is a flawed strategy.

We are 'Meaning Making Machines' (MMM). If we examine this in light of the caveman era, it all makes sense. We wouldn't survive long if we couldn't quickly assess a situation and take immediate action. Sabre-toothed tigers move quickly and we don't want to be the next meal. So it's not that we need to stop being 'Meaning Making Machines' (impossible to do anyway), we just need to realise that's what we do. And we could be totally wrong.

To be effective in my work, it's vital to get key points across. The inclusion of memorable images in my slide shows achieves this. One popular image depicts a peaceful rainforest scene (courtesy of the World Wildlife Fund). Participants are asked to describe what they see. Their tone often betrays their puzzlement at being asked such an obvious question. It's a rainforest ... clearly! With prompting, they look deeper. Finally, they see the snake, the elephant, the koala and her baby, the parrot, the crocodile, the wild boar, the lizard and all the cleverly camouflaged creatures hidden within. At the end of one such session, a participant scoffed "You are all delusional!" It was obvious he could only see the trees. How do you think that made him feel? His angry reaction appeared out of proportion to the situation. Yet, seen in the light of not being good enough or of not belonging, his reaction was understandable.

You're an idiot!

How about this one; you're driving along at the correct speed limit, when a car pulls out in front of you and starts travelling slower than the speed limit. You can't overtake this car and are forced to slow down. What do you think of the driver of the car in front? You're an idiot! Now you're driving along, again at the speed limit, when a car from behind speeds up and overtakes you. What do you think of the driver in that car? You're an idiot! This is a great example of how we expect others to do exactly what we're doing, because our way is the right way. The vast majority of people believe they are good drivers. It's everyone else who is doing the wrong thing.

The ABC Triangle

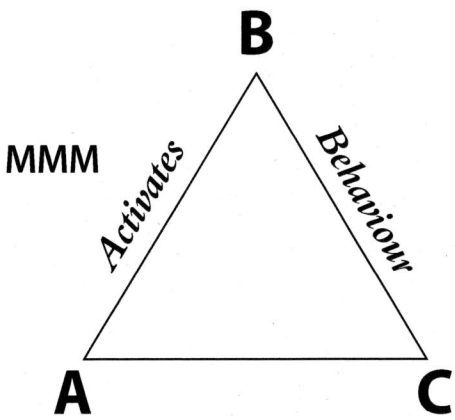

The ABC Triangle clearly illustrates how our beliefs impact our life.

Please write the word Action next to the A point of the triangle.

Action stands for the thing that happens, the event you see and/or hear that causes you to react in some way.

The B stands for Beliefs, now write that in too.

Whenever you see or hear an action, it activates a belief you hold around that action. For instance, say someone calls out "Nice day!" as they walk by. If you also believe it is a nice day, you may respond with a smile or agree by calling out, "Yes it sure is." If you've had an unhappy start to your day, perhaps you haven't noticed how beautiful the weather is. Therefore your response will be different, perhaps a 'not happy Jan' grumpy face. What if someone walks by and just glares at you? Instantly, that action activates your belief around what a 'glare stare' means.

As you already know, 'MMM' stands for 'Meaning Making Machines'. As 'Meaning Making Machines' we instantly give meaning to a given situation. If we believe our safety is threatened, we launch straight into our survival strategy. The red mist descends, the heat rises and our heart pounds as we breathe in a shallow, fast tempo. In that state, we're unable to reason logically so leap straight into an emotional moment.

That's what 'Action activates Belief' means.

Now write Consequences next to the 'C'.

So here we are, heart pounding, shallow breath, red mist descending and the heat rising. In that emotional state, we determine our behaviour. Often, that behaviour is not appropriate. Sound familiar? It is absolutely true our behaviour then determines the consequences. Under the word 'Consequences' write 'Bitter or Better?'

You can choose the consequence

Let's say you have a decision to make. As you ponder what to do, you are well aware the consequence for you will be bitter or better. (Not talking illegal or harmful to yourself or others.) What would you choose: bitter or better? When asking this question in my workshops everyone votes for a 'better' consequence. Dumb question right? However, think now of a decision you've made in the last month. Your decision determined whether the consequences would turn out bitter or better. What did you choose? Most people realise they chose bitter.

Why would any sane, normal person choose a consequence that ended up bitter for them? That's the point, when we've launched into the emotional side of our brain; we are not sane or normal. How often have you looked back at a decision you made and regretted it? It all happened so quickly. Sadly, some compound the issue by a deep need to be right.

It's how you respond

This quote by Amy Carmichael serves as a wonderful reminder of that choice.

"No difficulty that you ever face can of itself affect you: it is only your response to these things that will make you bitter or better."

Aha! I can almost hear your thoughts. So, you're saying it is our response to what happens that matters, not what actually happens? That's exactly the point, and not just my point either. Many teachers in the personal development sphere make the same point. Last year, I trained a group of regular Army, Air Force and Naval officers and soldiers. There's always push back on this 'Bitter or Better' concept and this military group assertively rose to the challenge. "What if you ended up in a wheelchair, how can that be better?" one officer shouted. Thankfully, due to recently reading a report on young men who were now living life in a wheelchair, I easily answered his question.

Carry on moaning or move on?

Here's the thing, you have the choice of forever moaning about how bad life is, or you can decide to accept what's happened and do the best you can: Bitter or better? One of these young men actually stated his life was better since his accident. As I couldn't imagine losing the use of my legs, this was a tough one to swallow. However, he went on to describe his life before the accident. As a good mechanic, he earnt big money then spent it all on gambling, drinking and sex workers. That was his life day after day, drifting with no purpose. You won't be surprised to hear he didn't have a girlfriend. Although it took some time to adjust, he's glad the accident happened. He travels a lot now, sharing messages of hope with other young people in wheelchairs. He believes his life has purpose and significance. And guess what? Yes, he has a girlfriend.

Your life is in your hands

This story so clearly illustrates the quality of your life rests in your hands and your hands alone. You can choose to attach an empowering meaning to whatever happens in your life, or not. You decide the consequence you'd prefer: Bitter or better.

We all have something that can never be taken away from us. That something is free will. Okay, if you're doped to the eyeballs with drugs, perhaps there's not much free will going on. Don't allow yourself to get to this state. Don't give your power away just because a person is wearing a white coat, or a suit or a beguiling smile. You have free will, so use it.

Back to our ABC Triangle.

The ABC Triangle illustrates the dynamics of how we react to life's circumstances.

1. An Action happens.
2. This action activates our Beliefs around what that means. If we interpret that action as threatening, our survival strategy is launched. Whilst in that emotional state, we decide our behaviour.
3. Our behaviour determines the Consequences: Bitter or Better?

The Vicious Triangle

This triangle now turns into the Vicious Triangle. Here's why. Remember Mary and her entrance into the lunchroom at the exact time her team members burst into laughter? This activated a belief Mary had about herself as not belonging. As a result, Mary experienced deep hurt. Instantly, she launched into her survival strategy and chose actions that resulted in an unpleasant environment for the whole team. The consequence was her team didn't want her around. Mary created her self-fulfilling prophecy. That's the vicious part. As Mary creates the bitter consequence, she feels justified in saying, "Look, I was right! I don't belong." Mary can now only see behaviour that supports her belief she doesn't belong. She remains blind to the empathy Anne showed.

What can you change?

Looking at the three parts to this triangle, you have the power to change only one of them. You cannot change the Action. It's already happened. It does no good to stamp your foot and say, "That shouldn't have happened!" The only part you have the power to change is Belief. It is imperative to discover what your beliefs around life are. If you don't, you will always be a piece of flotsam and jetsam on the sea of life. I get motion sickness just thinking about that.

Focus on what you can control. Recognise you are the one in control of your emotional state. Master your emotions and you will become master of your life. Am I saying stop being human, stop feeling and caring? Absolutely not! What I'm saying is you add little value to your situation when you decide to vomit over everyone. Refuse to ride the emotional roller coaster. Your emotions are triggered by what you believe is true. Eighty per cent of where you are in life right now is a result of your beliefs.

Don't unbuckle your seatbelt

Finding your beliefs

Here's an activity that will help identify those beliefs you hold so dear. Carry around a small notebook. Every time you hear yourself say something derogatory about yourself, regardless of whether it's in jest, take out that notebook and write it down. Whatever pops up in your mind, write it down. Become aware of what you say to yourself. If you're feeling bad, it's almost guaranteed to be a reaction to a thought you had. These thoughts are filtered through the beliefs we hold about life and ourselves. They flit through our mind so quickly we miss them. Start picking them up, because those automatic thoughts are running and ruining your life. Do this for a full month, checking your list every seven days. If you commit to doing this, you will be shocked at how often you put yourself down. There's no need to get upset when others do it because we're pretty good at doing it to ourselves.

In a recent workshop, a wonderfully witty woman called out, "I'm such an idiot!" As we'd just worked through The ABC Triangle I called her on that statement. She quickly got annoyed and pouted, saying she was only joking. Persisting, I asked her to write those words in her notebook. At the end of seven days, I guarantee she will be shocked at how often she puts herself down. And don't forget, your body is listening. Remember the results of Dr Masaru Emoto's experiments with water? Be aware.

How true is this little ditty:

Watch your beliefs for they become thoughts.
Watch your thoughts for they become words.
Watch your words for they become actions.
Watch your actions for they become habits.
Watch your habits for they become character.
Watch your character for it becomes your destiny.

Remember that personal development seminar I went to three decades ago 'Change Your Mind; Change Your Life'? Finally, I get how true this is. You will only change your life by changing your mind. Changing your mind means examining those beliefs you've grown up with and deciding if they're still useful to you as an adult.

Change your mind; Change your life – go on, I dare you.

"We either make ourselves miserable or we make ourselves strong. The amount of work is the same." – Carlos Castaneda

HOW Chapter 17:
The Word Hidden In Belief – Three Rays of Light

1. For many years I believed my lacklustre life was not my fault. It was the fault of annoying elements in the external world. Take responsibility for the results in your life. Get into the driver's seat. The view is so much better.
2. If your body could talk, what would it say to you?
3. Please ponder the reality of the Vicious Triangle. If this is your only take away from this entire book, both your time and money have been well spent.

Identify Your Ray of Light: take a moment to write down what you got from this chapter:

_____

_____

Summary

- If you can change your mind, you can change your life.
- Personal development seminars only work if you take action.
- Truly decide to do something internally, completely and totally and you are unstoppable.
- Hold the consequences of doing something in one hand and the consequences of not doing something in the other, then decide which is most important.
- Beliefs are a mental attitude of acceptance without proof.
- Beliefs are your mindset and determine your course through life.
- Nought to seven is the 'imprint period' where we soak up many of our beliefs.
- What do you automatically do, without thinking about the consequences?
- Battling your strongly held beliefs will mean struggling against cognitive dissonance.
- As it turns out the word belief also contains the word 'lie' – a belief can be a lie.
- The two most common beliefs about life; I'm not good enough and I don't belong.
- You have the power to change the landscape of your life.
- Wanting to belong is a powerful human need.
- Don't let 'beliefs' tell the story about circumstances you're only half aware of.
- We think we're always right. Sometimes we're not.
- It's not the action that causes the consequence, it's how we respond.
- Watch your beliefs because they eventually lead to your destiny.

Chapter 18

This Is Your Life:
HOW I GOT HERE

How did you get to where you are in your life right now? Looking back on Part Two, and considering all the events and elements that have conspired to shape your life so far, this chapter has to be written by you.

Please take the time to jot down your thoughts and feelings after reading this part. Were you born into a pink world and how has that affected your life's journey? Have you been afflicted by the curse of your comfort zone? How has not speaking your truth affected your life or the life of others? Did you discover your survival strategy? And how did you feel about the two most commonly held beliefs?

Part Two is meant to be a wake-up call to reveal those elements in your life that contributed to how you got here. No one else gets to see your words.

This is your life ... so write:

_____

_____

_____

_____

_____

Please do not continue to PART THREE until you've emptied your mind onto this page. Doesn't need to make sense, just do it! You may need to use extra sheets of paper. Keep writing until there is no more to write.

Finally, this space is for identifying just one thought from all you've written in Chapter 18. As you read through your own words, what is the most important, most compelling, most revealing thing you've written? What jumps out and surprises or shocks you? It may be an uncomfortable truth. Good, delight in that for designing a new life begins with awareness of the old.

"Out with the old, in with the True." – Jeff Brown

"What if you wake up one day and
you're 65 or 75, and you never got your memoirs
or book written or you didn't go swimming in
warm pools and oceans all those years because your
thighs were jiggly and you had a nice, big comfortable
tummy or you were just so strung out on
perfectionism and people pleasing, that you forgot to
have a big juicy, creative life of imagination and radical
silliness staring off into space like when you were
a kid? **It's going to break your heart.**
Don't let this happen. Pick a new direction, one you
wouldn't mind ending up at, and aim for that.
Shoot the moon."

-Anne Lamott

PART THREE:
WHAT I WANT

This is it, the big part. No way forward can be crafted if we don't know what we want. And, even more importantly, why we want to go there. As women over 60, what *do* we want out of life? Your job is to decide what *you* want. Sitting there, pen poised, what would you write on that blank sheet of paper; how would you answer that question? Is it to have more courage, more confidence and more celebration of life?

Asking this question of a woman over 80, she took a few moments to answer. Finally, she looked up and whispered "I wish I'd had more control over my own life. I wish I'd stood up for myself more. I wish I'd done more of what I wanted to do."

Whilst she didn't answer my specific question, I got the message.

The truest, yet seemingly unattainable, answer to what we all want out of life is to be happy. Many books and seminars explain the so-called 'recipe for happiness'. When we look around, few people are genuinely happy. Sadly, that probably includes us.

PART THREE covers four strategies to help you get what you want. It also identifies how you sabotage yourself. We must constantly re-evaluate what we do, lest habits and past wisdom blind us to new possibilities. This journey requires self-discipline. Rediscover the exhilaration of self-discipline and how having it leads to a better life. Finally, it's about time isn't it? To step up and get into the driver's seat of your own life I mean.

"*It's only possible to live happily ever after on a day to day basis.*" – Margaret Bonnano

Chapter 19
Working Out Your 'Why'

If we don't have a compelling 'Why' for want we want, we'll run out of fuel and fail to reach our journey's end. A well-defined 'Why' gives you the power to leap tall buildings and tackle outrageous and courageous endeavours. Alas, no one can tell you what your 'Why' is. Guidance can be provided but the discovery must be yours. Your 'Why' might simply be to feel good, because when you feel good much is possible. Maybe your 'Why' needs to make you cry? Each of us has a picture, however vague, of what we'd like to accomplish before we die. That picture is your 'Why'.

If your 'vague picture' is almost invisible, how do you discover your 'Why'? Clues are everywhere if you but look. What is your passion in life? What activity causes you to lose yourself? You know, those activities when hours whiz by in minutes. What excites you about life? Some women have looked me in the eye and muttered nothing excites them about life. Don't we all know someone who's walking around dead at 60? And sadly, zombies can be much younger than 60.

Discovering our 'Why' uncovers the vision we choose to accomplish in our lifetime. Knowing this creates an extraordinary feeling of significance and purpose. Once we see our vision, it is possible to develop our mission, the steps needed to fulfil our Why, our very reason for being. Please know your 'Why' doesn't have to be static, something set in concrete, never to change. We change course many times during our lifetime.

To live a big, juicy, creative life of
imagination and radical silliness

How wonderful is this 'Why'? See how owning a 'Why' like this sets the needle on the compass? If this was your 'Why', when contemplating any decision all you need do is ask "Does this support me to live a big, juicy, creative life of imagination and radical silliness?" Your 'Why' cannot be too big or too crazy. You'll know when you've discovered your 'Why'. You'll feel it, deep inside. It's when something wells up and fills you, it just feels right.

Ask quality questions

It's true; the quality of your questions determines the quality of your life.

Here are two quality questions to help get clarity on your 'Why'.
1. Why am I doing this? (Why do I do what I do?)
2. What happened to me that created this passion to take what I do to the world? (What personal struggles have caused me to want to make things different?)

Make the time to go into a quiet space and allow authentic answers to surface. Not the answers that sound good or what you think you should say. So be brave, be vulnerable, be authentic and be human. The answers must come from your heart, not your head. Write your answers down.

(The author of these questions: Diana Alvear)

It's time to share my 'Why'

Why do I do what I do? I believe we do not have to live a life mapped out by others. We are taught there is only 'the' way. I remind people they have free will and guide them to see 'their' way. That is my joy.

What personal struggles have caused me to want to make things different? My daughter once told me "Mum you've always stood up for the underdog." The irony of this is for most of my life I've considered myself to be the underdog. As a single mother on a supporting parent pension, I struggled with low self esteem, paying the bills and isolation. Fortunately, the leadership training provided to all Australian Army Reserve soldiers opened up a whole new world for me. That training showed me another way to be, and I grasped that way with both hands.

Putting your 'Why' down on paper is most revealing. I've toyed with many possibilities. To save the planet, to help bring peace to our world, to fight injustice and cruelty, to provide strategies to help people cope with unrest, my list is long.

Then I remembered it all starts with me. As Ghandi said, "Be the change you want to see in the world." To make a difference, I need to create a life where I feel happy first. That happiness creates a vibration that spreads, infects and affects all those in my sphere of influence. And that's the best I can do. We do not need to save the planet. Gaia is capable of saving herself; we need to save our species. That starts with people taking responsibility for their own self first.

'Why' makes your life richer

Knowing your 'Why' has the potential to make your life more rich, intense and meaningful. In supporting you to achieve that, your 'Why' must be challenging. When you life has no challenge, it has no meaning. Your 'Why' gives you a reason to get out of bed every morning. Your 'Why' dictates how you will live, how you will love and eventually, how you will die. Your 'Why' defines your life.

Not having a 'Why' is the easiest way to sabotage the self. You will meander around, drifting aimlessly from this to that. Bright shiny objects will attract and distract you. Although that 'fun' has its place, it's shallow and short-lived. Life is meant to be more. There is a reason 'Why' you are alive.

<u>WHAT</u> Chapter 19:
Working Out Your 'Why' – Three Rays of Light

1. Each of us has a picture, however vague, of what we'd like to accomplish before we die. Can you see yours?
2. Define your 'Why'.
3. How does your 'Why' make you feel?

Identify Your Ray of Light: take a moment to write down what you got from this chapter:

_____

_____

Summary

- Work out your 'Why' so you remain motivated.
- Work out your 'Why' so you see a reason to live.
- Not having a 'Why' is the easiest way to self–sabotage.

Chapter 20

The Power Statement

You've no doubt said "It's the little things that count." I tend to agree, especially when referring to the Power Statement. The Power Statement starts with two potent little words. What you put after them determines your happiness in life.

You know the words: I AM ...

The words we add after those first two little words, decide our fate. I can prove that right now.

The Power Statement Exercise

Stage 1

In a moment (but not just yet) I'll ask you to write the words 'I am' on a blank sheet of paper. Then you'll go ahead and complete that sentence by emptying the contents of your mind onto that sheet of paper. Perhaps you'll write something like pretty, a woman, a mother, tall, short, happy, sad, amazing, a lover, a widow, tragic, broke, rich, grey, a babysitter, colourful and so on. Keep writing until not even one more word tumbles out to complete the sentence.

Now do Stage 1. Write until no more words or phrases pop into your mind.

Stage 2

When you cannot think of anything else to add to the words 'I am', that means you've come to a blank space. Your mind is a blank. You're probably quite confident there's nothing more you can add. However, I can guarantee that isn't true, so don't stop now. Continue by saying softly to yourself "I am ..." It won't be long before other words spring to mind. Leaving one blank space under the list you've already written, continue to list those new words and phrases. Keep writing until you can think of no other way to complete the sentence. When no other words come to mind, you've come to another blank space.

Now do Stage 2. Write until no more words or phrases pop into your mind.

Stage 3

You might think there's nothing more to add. However, like before, that isn't true so don't give up. Continue by saying softly to yourself "I am ..." It might take longer this time, but eventually other words and phrases will spring to mind. Leaving one blank space under the list you've already written, now continue with your list.

Finished? Are you sure? Are there no more words to tumble from your mind?

Some of you may've struggled with the third attempt to empty your mind. That's okay. One client, who wanted to go further, delved deeper by moving past four blank spaces. Gutsy woman, I say.

Now for the debrief

You've probably guessed the first words and phrases that tumble from your mind are the surface things that you believe define you. These are normally what society, friends and family dictate and what you accept. They are not the real you. They represent the mask you've worn for so long, mainly because of your need to fit in. This is not to say the words and phrases you first wrote down are not true. They absolutely are true according to the 'you' that's 'under the influence'. Remember, we're not talking about mind-altering substances when talking about being 'under the influence'. We're talking about being under the influence of others. Doing what we think others expect. After all if we don't do that, what would people think?

It follows then, the words you wrote down after the first blank space, are more true of who you really are. These words are likely to be more authentically you.

The third set of listed words and phrases, after the second blank space, is the most revealing of all. You may not actually like what came out. Reading those words may cause emotion to rise, either from happiness or sadness. The feeling of happiness may be a celebration of recognising the true you. The sadness may be an acknowledgement of the years you've spent in denial of your true self.

Your response to this exercise cannot be pigeonholed. At each stage, you alone must decide the meaning of your words.

Do you dare go deeper? Do you dare go through another blank space? I've not gone there myself. Three levels have been more than enough for me to gain insight into that which I'd kept hidden for so many years.

If you haven't done this exercise yet—go ahead and do it now.

You have nothing to lose and so much insight to gain.

When will the time be right to break free of the expectations and limitations of others? When will you decide it's okay to start living your own life? And more importantly, when will you break free from the limitations and expectations you've imposed on yourself? When would be a good time to start?

How your Power Statement shapes your life

As we know, it's our beliefs that determine our experience and therefore the quality of our life. Tracey grew up with a strong Power Statement "I am dumb." She'd believed it all her life, because it was true. Everybody knew it was true and Tracey was often ragged about it whenever she did dumb things. Which was often. Tracey never realised she was dumb until she went to school. As a young girl, she suffered from a lazy eye so wore unattractive, thick-lensed glasses. And sometimes she was a little clumsy, which always drew an audience. How the other kids laughed then, she was blonde after all. Tracey grew up believing she was dumb. Even though it was never proven to be true, somehow it stuck. Whenever she did something that others got away with, Tracey never could. She often felt humiliated and ashamed. So she learnt to laugh at the comments and decided it didn't matter that she was dumb. However, as a 70-year-old-woman, Tracey still remembers she was always the dumb kid at school. As a 70-year-old woman, with deep wisdom gleaned from the rich tapestry of her life, Tracey still feels dumb.

Even on her deathbed, Tracey will still feel dumb. That's the saddest part; it doesn't have to be that way.

I am a diabetic

Be very careful how you finish the sentence beginning with "I AM ..."

Especially (for example) if you are inclined to say "I am a diabetic." You may have that disease, but it is not you. Do not make the mistake of identifying with diabetes so strongly that it becomes your identity. That is dangerous. Do not 'become' any disease or sickness; do not lose yourself.

Step into genuine curiosity and make a determined effort to notice your language around "I AM." Decide to use more empowering words. Have fun with this. When someone asks how you are, say 'I am epic!" Or perhaps "I am sensational!" or my favourite "I am fabulous! Thank you for asking." Notice how many people respond with "I am okay." Really ... is that all?

Be clear on how you use the Power Statement. It has the power to destroy your dreams. Happiness doesn't just happen. It is a condition that must be cultivated and you must be a dedicated gardener. The weeds will constantly threaten your garden so commit to vigilantly pulling them out.

Remember, the outcome is a choice, and the choice is always yours: Bitter or Better?

<u>WHAT</u> Chapter 20:
The Power Statement – Three Rays of Light

1. Write here one thing you got out of completing the Power Statement exercise:

_____

2. Tracey isn't the only child scarred by school life. Due to living on an island for many years, I developed a somewhat free spirited nature. When my family moved back to the mainland, it felt alien to wear shoes, even at school. I was 11 years old when paraded in front of the entire primary school assembly. My public humiliation was assured as the teacher reprimanded me for not wearing shoes. That was decades ago, but I still remember how that felt. Do you have a story to tell?
3. Choose right now a different response to the question "How are you?"

Identify Your Ray of Light: take a moment to write down what you got from this chapter:

_____

_____

Summary

- The words we add after "I am ..." decide our fate.
- These power statements, particularly the later ones, are the real you.
- Break free of the expectations of others and start living.
- Happiness doesn't just happen.

Chapter 21

The Finger Of Blame

This is a favourite topic. In my Leadership workshops, it's essential to discuss how pointing the Finger of Blame creates distrust. It's also a prime cause of plummeting morale. The same thing happens with friends and family. Yet, pointing the finger of blame is so much a part of our society, many aren't even aware they're doing it. In case you're not aware of how this looks, let's do it right now.

Let's do it!

Pick up your hand and point your forefinger straight out in front. Imagine you're pointing this finger at someone who's not done the right thing by you. Yes, they're to blame. They made you do it, look bad, lied to you or any number of guilty actions. Okay that was fun, and didn't they deserve it. Now we need to look at our hand, the one still pointing that finger of blame. Notice how many fingers are pointing back at you. Yes, three fingers are pointing right back at you, and there's a good reason why.

Consider this, if you're involved in drama it's because you've played a part in it. You're a part of it because of something you did not do, that you should have done, or something you did do that you should not have done.

You can't change others

Here's why 'Pointing the finger of blame' is so damaging to you. We've already agreed you cannot change any other person (not even your children). You cannot reach inside a person, twist their guts and mess with the chemicals of their brain to get them to think differently about something. That's an internal job they must do themselves. We cannot change any other person.

The only person you can change is the one sitting in your seat.

You may be pointing the finger at someone else, but those three fingers pointing back at you are to remind you of your part in this play of life.

So, by pointing the finger of blame at our kids, our boss, our mother, our council, our government and yes, even aliens, we doom ourselves to victimhood. We doom ourselves to a position where life can't get any better. A sad fate awaits Kate who declares Jenni must change, because it's her fault. Kate stews on the problem and cannot see a way out of the dark place. Meanwhile, Jenni is out dancing.

Use the three fingers

Instead of dwelling in this dark place, look at those three fingers pointing right back at you. Be prompted to ask yourself what are three steps you can take towards a solution. Any question will do. How about this one? "What is it I can change in my life right now, to get a better result?" Decide on three steps, and take them.

We point the finger of blame when we're not happy about how something has turned out and are not prepared to own our part in it.

Here's a good example of a woman who continued to complain loud and long about her miserable situation. Habitually pointing the finger of blame means she does not acknowledge it is in her power to change her experience of that situation.

Sarah's Story

Sarah lived in the country and was most unhappy in her job with a local council. During the entire six hour workshop, she continually sniped at her boss and co-workers. She often stated a situation 'shouldn't' be happening. Finally, I challenged her to consider the options she can take to change her life.

Here is the model we worked through:

<u>Your Three Life Options</u> (We always have three options to consider, always)

1. Change It!
2. Accept It!
3. Leave It!

First, can Sarah Change It? Sarah said No! She'd tried everything and nothing had worked. Remember, the change has to be around the processes, not the people because it is not possible to change others (although we can influence them).

So we looked at the option to Accept It! "NO! I cannot accept it, it's unfair." Sarah yelled.

That leaves us Option 3 to Leave It! "I can't leave it!" Sarah moaned. I live in this small country town and I'll never get another job here."

Okay, that takes us back to Option 1. Sarah was asked if she was absolutely sure she couldn't change the situation. "Fat chance of that." Sarah said.

Sarah now has to seriously look at her options. She is adamant she cannot Leave It! Therefore, the only workable option, in her case, is to Accept It!

Acceptance helps

Here's the weird thing. If Sarah decides to Accept It (and truly does accept it) her attitude will change. It cannot stay the same. Once Sarah stops kicking and screaming about all the bad bits, she might see the good bits she's been blind to. If we live our lives looking at only the bad, we are blind to the good.

If we truly always have these three options in life, consider them when you next say to yourself and others, I didn't have an option. You always do; you just don't like the consequences of the other options. So you settle. Whichever option you choose, there is a consequence. That's life right?

If you've worked through the three available options and decided the consequences of one of them works best for you, then step into it. Take action, do something different. We're so afraid sometimes of stepping out, of jumping off the edge.

Are you a whinger?

If you are, stop whinging about your current situation. If you're not prepared to exercise your power to change that situation, then so be it! But stop whinging about it. This is the quickest way to lose respect and friendships. Decide it's your choice to accept it, because it is your choice. Be determined to find something positive, something good. And even if you can't do that, and you decide to stay in that situation, know it is your decision to stay. Own that decision. Don't 'should' on people; they should do this or should do that. That's expecting them to change and live life the way you believe it should be lived. We've already had that conversation. Decide to do something or do nothing, either way it's your choice. Own that.

Take back your power

Notice the times you do point the finger of blame, notice the three fingers pointing back at you and decide, or not, to do something about it. Own your decision, your choice. You may be thinking about my statement concerning the three life choices. Perhaps you're thinking about someone in jail, they don't have three choices. And you're right there of course. Or are you? Let's work through the three.

1. Change It! They could attempt to escape (not recommended). Perhaps the only thing they can change is their treatment by being a model prisoner. As a model prisoner, they might get early parole.
2. Accept It! This is a given. If you don't accept the reality of the situation you are setting yourself up for a very nasty time. It could be that 'not accepting' a situation may be the very reason they're in prison.
3. Leave It! Only at Her Majesty's Pleasure. True, this is the least likely option in this scenario. I guess it all depends on what one's interpretation of 'Leave It!' is. Taking your own life is 'leaving this mortal plane.'

The real point here is to realise one could've thought through the three options prior to doing the crime, so not ended up doing the time.

<u>WHAT</u> Chapter 21:
The Finger Of Blame – Three Rays of Light

1. Are you prone to pointing the Finger of Blame?
2. The Finger of Blame is a great tool to show children the consequences of doing so. As you're explaining this concept, actually get them to point their finger too.
3. Please remember the three options you always have: Change it! Accept it! Or Leave it! As expected, there are consequences to each one. Consider carefully.

Identify Your Ray of Light: take a moment to write down what you got from this chapter:

_____

_____

Summary

- If you're involved in drama it's because you have played a part in it.
- The only person you can change is the one sitting in your seat.
- Ask yourself, "What is it I can change in my life right now, to get a better result?"
- You can change it, accept it, or leave it.
- Notice when you're whinging. Then stop whinging!

Chapter 22
The Older And Bolder Blessing

"*I did not find myself until I turned 80.*" Ilona Royce Smithkin (94 years old) Star of the movie *Advanced Style*

I LOVE BEING OVER 60! There's absolutely no way I'd swap that which I hold in my head and my heart for fewer wrinkles and firmer skin. Five decades ago, I remember listening to mum talking to her friends as they played cards. Reminiscing on her youth, Mum would say "If only I knew then what I know now." All sounded a bit like gobbledegook to the teenager me.

Now, it all makes sense. How dangerous would our young people of today be if they knew what we know now? If you've seen the movie 'The Matrix', you'll remember how Keanu Reeve's character could be plugged into all available knowledge. In nanoseconds, he learnt how to expertly fly a helicopter. How much fun would that be? Perhaps one day, the young will possess the wisdom of the ages. The merging of years of experience with innocence and youthful beauty would create compelling and dynamic beings. In a reality like that, where would the aged and their wisdom fit in? Certainly wouldn't be as elders of their time, no further need for that.

We've earnt our wrinkles

Now back to reality. I tell people I've earnt these wrinkles and it's true. Sure, there are days when I look in the mirror and feel shocked at the rapidly increasing signs of age. What to do? One could always resort to injecting Botox to erase the wrinkles. Yes, and there are other procedures to trick the reflection in the mirror. But drastic trickery it is. Time will eventually reveal the consequences of injecting poison into your skin. That path is not mine, although every woman has the right to decide if it is hers.

Older is reality

Being older and bolder may not resonate as a true blessing. But here's the thing, being older is the reality. That lined face staring back at me in the mirror is part of my physical body. Even though the visual doesn't define the totality of who I am, it's what others see. Chasing a youthful exterior is a futile journey. You may disagree, but hear me out. Ageing is the natural progression of our physical journey. Yes, factors hasten the ageing process and we don't have control over many of them. However, we can control our choices over factors like smoking, drinking alcohol or moving our bodies on a regular basis. Every single day we make numerous, seemingly small decisions that impact how we end those days. We have the power to assess each decision, to determine the impact on our well-being. No pill or procedure has the ability to replicate our effervescence, our vitality, our true inner beauty. Yes, I know you're groaning at that time-worn cliché. And I understand why. We give so much of our power away by succumbing to decisions made by those labelled as experts. Even after all these years, many still believe the TV advertising mandate on how we should look, of how our lives should be. Consider the impact celebrity culture has on so many lives today. I lament the slavish adherence to the 'words of wisdom' handed down by film, pop and TV stars – especially when they serve as role models for younger women. This opportunity to truly and profoundly influence many generations is squandered. All in the name of advertising and what will make the most money. Luckily, we do have some wonderful female celebrity role models.

> **True inner beauty is imprisoned by the very denial it exists.**

Exist it does. When we claim our wisdom, our worth, our right to have a say in the ways of our world, only then is our inner beauty set free. It emanates through sparkling eyes, lighting our face and straightening our stature.

Embrace or run?

The older and bolder blessing is manifold. It includes the ability to choose our feelings and to positively embrace our reality. It took time, but now we know we create our reality. We've always created our reality by reacting how we have and choosing to believe what we do. Finally, we see that so can boldly step into living a better life, a life we'd prefer. Yes, it takes courage and confidence to do that.

If *we* don't, who will?

Or we can choose to fight against the flow of life, the rhythm of our advancing years. We can prefer to look into the mirror and hate our reflection. We weep over this inevitable cruel process stealing our youth. Blinded by our tears we fail to see the damage our anguish and despair inflicts on our bodies. This anguish and despair sits as a dark rock in our gut, creating a state of deep unhappiness and unease. Bitter or better? As always, the choice rests squarely on our shoulders.

When we smile, when we feel joy, when we celebrate our worth and the value of our wisdom, when we develop the moral courage to stand for what we believe, only then do we take our rightful place in society as an 'Elder of Our Time'. Carpe Diem.

<u>WHAT</u> Chapter 22:
The Older And Bolder Blessing –
Three Rays of Light

1. Is older and bolder a blessing? Please explore the reason for your response.
2. Personal grooming takes effort and time. I place a high priority on personal grooming and have fun playing around with different looks. For some women, personal grooming activities score low on their list of priorities. There is no right or wrong, there is only choice and the consequences of that choice.
3. Do not be defined by others, especially those who stand to make money from your preferences. Be courageous. Be confident. Be you.

Identify Your Ray of Light: take a moment to write down what you got from this chapter:

_____

_____

Summary

- We've earnt our wrinkles and deeply etched life lines.
- Ageing is a reality and no amount of denial will change the outcome.
- The beauty within may be a cliché but we make it true by accepting who and what we are and letting that confidence resonate on the outside.
- Will you be bitter or better about the ageing process?

Chapter 23
This Is Your Life: WHAT I WANT

What do you want out of life right now?
Looking back on Part Three, and considering all those events and elements that've conspired to shape your life so far, this chapter has to be written by you.

Please take the time to jot down your thoughts and feelings after reading this part.

Consider the following as you write. Have you always known your 'Why' or are you yet to discover it? What has been your most used Power Statement? How has that worked for you? We all point The Finger of Blame; how has doing that affected your life? Will you stop doing that? Is 'the Older and Bolder Blessing' a myth?

Part Three is a wake-up call, revealing elements that define what you want out of life. No one else gets to see your words. This is your life ... so write:

Please do not continue onto PART FOUR until you've emptied your mind onto this page. It doesn't need to make sense, just do it! You may need to use extra sheets of paper. Keep writing until there is nothing more to write, until your mind is a blank.

Finally, this space is for identifying just one thought from all you've written above. As you read through your own words, what is the most important, most compelling, most revealing thing you've written that jumps out and surprises or shocks you? It may be an uncomfortable truth. If it is, delight in that for designing a new life begins with awareness of the old.

"Out with the old, in with the True." – Jeff Brown

"Do not FEAR.

Look beyond what's dying

to what's being born."

Marianne Williamson

How To Make The Rest Of Your Life THE BEST *Of* YOUR LIFE

PART FOUR:
WILL TAKE ACTION

How to make the rest of your life the best of your life: You must have the confidence and the courage to choose the road to take, the detours to make, the scenery to admire, when to stop and when to rest. It's your foot that needs to be on the pedal and your hands on the steering wheel. But if you don't turn the key, nothing changes. You'll stay right where you are. So buckle up and get into Drive because action changes everything. Yet many refuse to take positive action to change their lives because of a four-letter word: FEAR.

PART FOUR examines why your best bet may be to jump off the edge, to determine if you have the will to take action. We look at why it's vital to plan your life and not just your holiday. Next we tackle how to set goals and whether or not we deserve to achieve our goals. Do you know the real secret to achieving your goals? This part provides specific techniques for giving effective feedback. To do this well, you need to look at your communication skills. And we dive deeper into why women don't ask.

Chapter 24
The Rabbit In The Middle Of The Road

And that's exactly what it felt like. It was dark and I was staring wide-eyed at the car headlights rapidly approaching. My heart constricted with fear, my limbs were frozen and my mind screamed. For a brief moment, I saw myself as the rabbit in the middle of the road, blinded by the headlights of an unimaginable fate and unable to save myself. It was a scary, paralysing moment.

Have you ever felt like this? It wasn't that long ago I felt exactly like this.

Not smart

As a single woman with over 60 years of smarts, I certainly didn't feel smart for finding myself in a fearful, yet avoidable, situation. The problem was I didn't have the available cash to pay next month's rent. The telephone and energy bills were banging on my door too. Not to mention those demanding credit card payments. I was embarrassed. How did I let myself get into this situation? It really wasn't very smart at all, yet I considered myself to be a smart woman. Clearly I was delusional.

My mind searched for a solution. Perhaps I could borrow the money? Being a woman of my era, it's easy to give but not so easy to take. Ego gets in the way there. I couldn't ask. Besides, I shouldn't need to ask. Even though I'm not extravagant, the recriminations began as I remembered spending money, perhaps unwisely.

Since starting my own training business six years ago, I've invested over $65,000 in training courses and seminars to continue to grow my knowledge and competence. Whilst nothing is ever a total waste of money because some benefit is always gained, it's been a mostly sorry experience of unfulfilled promises. For example, I clearly remember one 'guru' saying, "Victoria, if you don't make your money back in two weeks, I'll give you a full refund." I cringe as I remember his words, because I believed them.

However, please don't think I'm pointing the Finger of Blame. I chose to do those courses. I chose to slap my credit card down. As integrity is my top business value, I've certainly learnt how to offer courses with integrity. And that has to be a good thing. So what to do?

Perhaps, I said to myself, you should listen to your own words:

The quality of your life is determined by the quality of your questions.

How true this is. Have you ever said to yourself "What's wrong with me?" Having an obedient and clever mind, your question will be answered within microseconds. Clear evidence of the multitude of things wrong with you will flood into your head. The bonus will be you get to feel even worse. Why don't we ask the more empowering question "What's right with me?" Really, why do we never ask that question?

So I asked this quality question "What is it I'm not seeing?" Another way to ask "What am I missing?"

The get out of jail phone call

Due to my sombre state, it was important to sit with this question. It took a while, but eventually I queried why an important phone call had not been made. No, my mind argued, you already know what their answer will be. There has to be another way! But the thought persisted and dominated my headspace until I decided to make that clarifying phone call. Early next morning, I dialled the number and heard four little words that changed everything. I cried with relief as the weight lifted from my shoulders. Later that day I wondered, what if I'd not made that phone call? Would I've found another way to get out of jail?

Regardless of the answer, I needed to stay out of jail. This entailed a tough love look at where my life was headed. It wasn't pretty. It was clear current strategies weren't working. Taking a big breath, I put on my big girl panties and summoned up the courage to let go of a major client. As a fellow baby boomer, you know we cling to security. As I've already shared, this major client gave me lots of work; my calendar was full and I was busy. However, it's a dumb strategy to be busy but not profitable. It should've been blindingly obvious. But I'd kept the faith, hoping it would turn around and get better. Instead, it got worse. Hindsight is a wondrous thing. Time to do something different.

> **Stop the same old, same old. Dare to do something different.**

The scared part

Every now and again, that part of me that's still scared rises up and asks, "What if this doesn't work out, what will you do then?" Again, I have a belief I always get by. No matter what happens, I always come up smelling of roses (excuse the pun). Living a fearful life shuts down your creativity. It shuts down your ability to see a better way, to live a better life. It hurts.

When you're frozen like a rabbit caught in the middle of the road, all you can see in the blinding headlights is the car registration plate: FEAR. If you don't summon up the will to take action, you'll be squished. Not my preferred outcome and I'm confident it's not yours either.

WILL Chapter 24:
The Rabbit In The Middle Of The Road –
Three Rays of Light

1. FEAR has two useful acronyms to help rise above this de-bilitating state. Choose one that works best for you: False Evidence Appearing Real; Face Everything And Rise. Then there's this one: Forget Everything And Run

2. At my age, I certainly felt shame for sliding into a desper-ate financial mess. My gambler type hopes of it all turning around, without taking specific action to address the mess, was a typical 'ostrich head in the sand' tactic. It's no comfort to know I'm far from the only baby boomer experiencing this.

3. Please never ask yourself "What's wrong with me?" The bo-nus of asking this is you get to feel worthless. Nothing is wrong with you! Your strategies might need tweaking or overhauling, but nothing is wrong with *you*. Everyone has the ability to get back on track, if they choose to. Sometimes we forget how resourceful we really are.

Identify Your Ray of Light: take a moment to write down what you got from this chapter:

_____

_____

Summary

- The quality of life is determined by the quality of your questions.
- Ask yourself 'What's right with me?' rather than the usual, 'What's wrong with me?'
- Don't do the same old, same old and expect a different result.

Chapter 25
Chart Your Own Life RoadMAP

It's never too late to look at where you're going and decide you don't want to go there. Don't you agree? Your Life RoadMAP lays out the destination of your choice

It also details the step-by-step route to get there. In this chapter, you see how to do just that whilst building on the treasure buried in the previous chapters. Every single chapter in this book contains a nugget of gold. The nugget of gold you unearthed in one chapter may be different to the one unearthed by another reader. My intention is to bury more than one nugget of gold within these words, but whatever you found is right for where you are right now.

Unearth this nugget of gold

Imagine walking into a travel agency and saying "I want to go overseas for two weeks later this year." The travel agent asks "When would you like to go?" You say "Oh, anytime. It doesn't matter when I go." Surprised at your answer, the agent cautiously enquires "Where would you like to go?" "Oh, anywhere!" you shout happily. It's unlikely anyone would do that right? Many details need to be organised before you travel: passports, visas, credit cards, mountains or beach or both, sun or snow? Who will look after your pet, water your plants, check the mail and so the list grows. How is it we go to great lengths to carefully plan our holiday, yet fail to plan our life?

A self-fulfilling prophecy

No one likes to fail; I think most people would agree with that. So they ask "Why bother to map out my life's plan, it won't work. Nothing turns out the way I want." Yes, it is tricky. But making goals and planning a strategy to get there is the best use of your time. And yes, expect that plan to fail. It's a military truism that no plan survives the first battle. No matter how carefully we plan our two-week holiday, rarely does it turn out exactly as we'd imagined. So, if two weeks proves difficult to plan what hope do we have planning an entire lifetime? Therefore, setting goals and planning life is a waste of time. No. Fail to plan then plan to fail. Behold, the prophecy is fulfilled. Absolutely nothing will turn out the way you wanted.

It's true your written-down life plan will more than likely fail, even at the first step. I'm here to tell you that it doesn't matter! Here's why. Other possible courses of action open up only after you've taken the first step. Standing outside the situation, one does not have the 'sight' to see all possible options. Hindsight is the understanding of a situation or event only after it has happened or developed. That's why we say hindsight is a good thing, but it cannot happen until you've taken action. Some say any action is better than no action; this may be true too. Personally, I believe taking the time to plan appropriate action is hugely beneficial. Before I share why, let's first look at the overview, often called the flow, for achieving what you want in life.

An overview for achieving your goals

Decide your goal, plan each step to achieve that goal, take action, be open to feedback, if not on target, assess then take the next logical step.

1. <u>Goal</u> – decide: no goal can be scored without knowing the whereabouts of the goal posts. When we know what we're aiming for in life, life changes. That conversation we overheard at our favourite café, normally we'd ignore it, but not this time. Because we know what we want, our ears pricked up when we heard talk about a new idea. We instantly saw that new idea could help us reach our goal, so we listened in. Goals can be simple or complicated; the process to achieve them is the same. It's important to commit your goal to paper. Yes, you can use a Word document on your computer. But there's something about the physicality of working with

paper that enhances the writing experience. At the end of this chapter, you'll find a simple format for writing your goals. Seriously consider using this format. It's crafted in a way to set you up to have the best chance to achieve your goal.

2. Plan – step by step: what are all the little steps you must take to achieve your goal? One way to work out those steps is to imagine you've achieved the goal. Then see yourself standing in that place of achievement. Turn and look back on your journey. Imagine you can see all the steps you took to finally be in this place of success. Write those steps down. Laugh if you like, but this NLP strategy is extremely effective. Give it a go; see if it works for you.

   A clever goal commits to the precise date you intend to achieve it. Let's say you've decided it'll take 12 calendar months to do that. Commit to the exact day, month and year at the end of those 12 months. To support you in that commitment, here is another effective planning strategy. Most goals have subgoals. With a 12 calendar month timeframe, determine a subgoal to be achieved at the end of each three months. You'll end up with four subgoals. Now you need to figure out what steps are needed to achieve these four subgoals. Having a visual helps you keep track of where you are and where you need to be next. To do that, mark a calendar into three-monthly sections with a subgoal for each. (Depending on the timeframe of your end date, these four subgoals can run concurrently.) Each quarter/three-monthly section now has a subgoal. Looking at that sub-goal, you will see the steps needed to achieve it. Now make a sub-subgoal for each month. Completion of the sub-subgoals equals completion of the sub-goal. Completion of all four subgoals equals achievement of your main goal. This division method is an easier way to work out the steps to take. I know it looks complicated here, but take the time to draw it out and you'll see just how easy it is.

3. Action – take the first step: have the courage and confidence to boldly step into the journey. Don't be concerned if others laugh because you took a misstep.

4. <u>Feedback</u> – are you moving towards or away from your goal? Do not become discouraged if your first step didn't work. Few first steps do. Notice what happened, and be clear on the situation you now find yourself in.

5. <u>Assess</u> – adjust if necessary. Here's why I believe taking the time to plan appropriate action is hugely beneficial. Success is not a straight line. Benchmarking is a valuable tool to help you track that line. Benchmarking uses your original plan as a point of reference. Then adjustments are assessed based on what worked and what didn't. By doing this, you get to see just how curly that success line can be. Knowing what worked and what didn't gives you valuable insight into how you best achieve your goals.

How benchmarking works

Taking that first planned step gives you valuable feedback. Did it work? (Meaning, am I moving towards my goal?) Or not? (Meaning: am I moving away from my goal?) If you are moving towards your goal, take the second step. If you've moved away from your goal, time to assess and adjust. Can I see something I was blind to before? Is there a better way? Importantly, please remember success is not a straight line. Sometimes you'll move sideways.

> **Remember, she who laughs last laughs best.**

Sometimes it'll be necessary to step backwards. Notice, assess and adjust. This process repeats until you reach your goal. The interesting thing is, you may even change your mind about your goal during this journey. Nothing is set in concrete. Simply notice what works and what doesn't then rinse and repeat.

We're making goals all the time

You would've heard the oft-stated statistic on how most people don't have goals. And of those that do, many do not write those goals down. Do you have written down goals? You may be surprised to know some don't know how to make goals. Now that is surprising because we're making goals all the time. We don't call them goals though. When we organise to catch up for a coffee or drink, that's a goal. When we arrange to go to the movies with our friends, that's a goal. When we see a pair of shoes we must have, and decide to go without certain expenses until we can afford to buy them, that's a goal. To achieve any of these things, we have to plan. That could be to mark the social event in our calendar, or plan how much to save until we can pay for those shoes. We don't plan any other activity for those committed times. We've set a goal and we do our best to honour that intention.

Perhaps the word 'goal' doesn't work for you. Then think of it as 'intention' or 'outcome' or 'purpose' or any word that means your chosen destination for your life. Now that is a big goal! And when you think of it, every other goal we set is just a subgoal to help achieve that big goal. Would you purposefully choose to be flotsam and jetsam tossed around on the sea of life? I don't think so. Often we help others achieve their goals and forget we have a life too.

My abysmal failure

About three years ago, I discovered how good I was at writing down my goals. Browsing through an old notebook, I came across goals written almost 12 years ago. It's embarrassing to admit my abysmal failure at achieving any of those carefully written down five and ten year goals. My life didn't resemble, even vaguely, any of those intentions and desires from so long ago. And the two main reasons I never even came close to achieving those goals become perfectly clear. Let's look at the first reason.

Time to tackle deservability

One of the reasons we don't achieve our goals is we don't think we deserve them.

No matter how much I wanted that penthouse by the sea with the convertible in the undercover garage, did I deserve to have them? Surely that was just pie in the sky? Did I deserve to have matching accessories? Did I deserve to be loved? Who was I to desire such things, to rise above my station in life? What about the starving hordes in some third world country? Better to send money there rather than on one's selfish desires. This is known as 'The Guilt Trip'. Many of us have been on this road for years. Whether it is 'the guilt trip' or the 'I don't deserve that' trip, it's time to get off that road. It's never served you and it never will, unless you gain some enjoyment from feeling worth-less? Decide you do deserve, simply decide, because it's true. If that thought causes inner turmoil, sit with it and wonder why it does. You cannot achieve anything you want (this has to be what YOU want) if you don't think you deserve it. You will always sabotage yourself or allow others to do so. Has your life's journey been all about pleasing others at the expense of your dreams? Wake up! Wake up now ... and let go. Let go of that voice whispering you don't deserve to live a better life. When you decide you do deserve to live a better life, you shine a light so others see they can too.

The second reason my goals never had a chance of fulfilment will be covered in the next chapter.

<u>WILL</u> Chapter 25:
Chart Your Own Life RoadMAP –
Three Rays of Light

1. RoadMAP: Is the road you're travelling mapped out by you or another? MAP is the acronym for My Action Plan. If you don't set goals, when would be a good time to start? Determine your 'My Action Plan' for a 12-month goal. Your RoadMAP will detail your goal and your step-by-step plan to achieve it.

2. The format to write a goal for your MAP.
   IT IS ____ (state the exact date you intend to achieve your goal e.g. 12/12/15)
   I AM _____ (stated in the present tense, as though you have achieved your goal e.g. I am sitting in my red convertible driving along the boulevard.)

I KNOW I'VE ACHIEVED MY GOAL BECAUSE _____ (explain the experience of achieving your goal using as many of the senses as possible e.g. The wind is gently blowing my hair, the smell of new leather chairs envelopes me, I see my friends clapping, I feel the sun softly kissing my skin, etc.)

3. If you can imagine it, you can achieve it. Step-by-step action is the key to achieving your goal. Deservability is never an issue.

Identify Your Ray of Light: take a moment to write down what you got from this chapter:

_____

_____

Summary

- We plan mundane things, but not life.
- Make goals and have a strategy to achieve them.
- The plan may not survive the first event, but you always get valuable feedback.
- Planning of any sort helps you define and refine what you want.
- Goal, Plan, Action. Feedback, Assess.
- Success isn't a straight line.
- Decide you deserve the goals you set.

Chapter 26

The Fortune Is In Your Feelings

Women are often told they are too emotional, so how can the fortune be in our feelings? It's true the fortune is in the follow-up, but surely not in our feelings? Bear with me as I explain.

Most of us don't get to this fine age without having experimented with the odd philosophy or two. And you would've noticed there are a great many to choose from.

Many moons ago, a book called *The P'TAAH Tapes* helped me make sense of this journey called life. This was my first experience of a channelled book, and I couldn't put it down. So many answers to difficult life questions were discovered within the pages of *The P'TAAH Tapes*. Yet how could that be? Are we to believe an alien or otherworld entity can talk through a human? Surely this is a charade? It has to be a trick to divest fools of their money.

Always listen to the message

Luckily for me, my science fiction upbringing helped me see through the noise. Others laughed, but I listened to the message. Have you noticed how good we are at shooting the messenger? We even have a saying to prove that's what we're inclined to do, "Don't shoot the messenger." We shoot them or we idolise them. If we decide to idolise them first, they'll eventually fall from their pedestal, then we shoot them, or hang them or crucify them.

But back to the messages discovered in *The P'TAAH Tapes*. Those messages made sense and provided clear action steps. Sadly, in those days I knew no other person I could share these concepts with. This created a sense of isolation. It was awkward believing such different things to my family and friends. The courage part had to kick in here. It does take courage to follow your own path. However, you always know, deep inside, when you're on the right track. So I lived the learnings, slowly creating a better life for my children and for me.

The next revelation in channelled books came when I discovered Seth (channelled through Jane Roberts). Next came Abraham channelled through Esther Hicks.

Last year, Bashar was added to my library of channelled wit and wisdom. An American, Darryl Ankar, has channelled Bashar for 35 years now. Many videos are available on YouTube and are well worth watching. Bashar knows how to have a good belly laugh whilst imparting gems on how we can create a life we'd prefer.

Yes, there are others, but really, how many channelled entities do you need?

The reason I mention all these channelled books is to set the scene for the reason this chapter is titled *The Fortune is in Your Feelings*. Although this message is undoubtedly in other books I've read, sometimes you're not ready to see it or hear it. It's true 'When the student is ready the teacher appears'.

Why I never achieved those old goals

Various techniques are offered throughout my book to help you step into the driver's seat of your own life. The last chapter revealed the first reason why my five and twelve year goals were never realised. I felt I didn't deserve them.

The second reason for non-achievement of those old goals turns out to be equally as simple. This discovery happened recently whilst reading another Bashar book. In his book, Bashar revealed a technique I'd never heard of before, yet made so much sense. To explain that technique, we need to play a little game of imagining.

With fingers crossed, I'm hoping you've created your own RoadMAP. That means you've taken the time to map out your goal, the stops along the way, the detours, whether you'll take the high road or the low road and planned for unexpected events. When you do this and take steady action steps, you will finally reach your goal. There's no doubt that will happen. Imagine how incredibly fulfilling that will be. Take a moment to imagine how that will feel. You've taken the time it's taken, travelled with whomever you've decided can be your passengers for however long you wanted, and you did it. In your imagination, see yourself there, having achieved your goal. What smells delight you? Can you taste the sparkling champagne as you and your friends toast your success? What can you hear? Who else, if anyone, is there? What are you touching? What feelings are swirling around inside you? Feel all of that! Now turn it up and feel it even more. Turn up the volume, the sounds, the feelings, the smells and the tastes. Bring that image up real close and wrap it all around you and live the experience with every single fibre of your body. Wow! Now take a deep breath. Life is good.

Your feelings are key

If you trusted and followed my directions, you just had an intense, delicious experience. Your feelings, as you turned up the volume, are key to you living a better life. The life you deserve. There is no limit to the joy and delight possible when you imagine yourself achieving your goal. This I've known through my NLP practice, and it works. Your very being vibrates at such a high frequency; the joy can be almost unbearable. But we only anchor this wonderfully happy way of feeling to the achievement of our goal. Yes, it's good practice to review your written goal every day. And that means practising and anchoring that feel-good feeling. But it isn't enough.

The Bashar technique – The second reason

What if you decided to practise that delicious feeling of well-being many times a day? Why only reserve it for when you think of your goal? Doesn't it feel good to feel good more often? And that, my friends, is the final piece that will bring your good fortune to you. The secret to making your life the best it can be is to practise that delicious feeling of achieving your goal. Practise it in all its intensity and delight. Get good at feeling that way whenever you want. Snap your fingers and feel good instantly. Get good at this and your life will change. It cannot help but do so.

Here's why. When you feel good you're happy, you look happy, the sun shines from you and happy people are drawn to you. Opportunities will present themselves to you, as a magnet draws things to itself. Quantum science has proven all things vibrate. We vibrate at a certain speed when we're happy and at a different speed when we're sad. We've mentioned that misery loves company. Yes, but not the company of happy people. A miserable person sends out vibes to other miserable people as they moan, "Oh woe is me; what an unfair world we put up with." And the happy people stay away. Realise how good you feel when you imagine achieving your goal and decide to practise feeling that way all the time.

What if you decided to do only those things that brought you joy? Glancing down your to-do list, what if you prioritised that list based on what you'd actually like to do?

Brought back to earth!

Sharing this with a good friend, she brought me back to earth with a thud! Victoria she sighed, the toilets have to be cleaned sometimes. She's right of course. Thinking this through, I decided cleaning the toilet is a non joyful job that's made even more non joyful when approached with an icky attitude. Having an icky attitude when doing chores seems to make toilet cleaning more unbearable. When feeling good, one whizzes through the toilet cleaning. Well, that works for me.

After the ecstasy
The laundry!

— Jack Kornfield

All chores done w/ an attitude of
gratitude & deep heartfelt joy
become easy & pleasant. :)

<u>WILL</u> Chapter 26:
The Fortune Is In Your Feelings –
Three Rays of Light

1. Have you read any channelled books?
2. Were you able to imagine the full-on feeling of achieving your goal? We use mind imagery many times to create our experience of life. Most of the time, it's not for our good. We imagine what people say about us. We imagine what that look from our boss or loved one means. When we wake up in the early hours of the morning, our mind floods with images of 'stuff' we worry about. You have full ability to imagine 'stuff' that brings you joy, it just takes practise.
3. Notice when you don't feel good. You can change that emotion. Remember how it felt when you imagined reaching your goal? Decide to imagine that.

Identify Your Ray of Light: take a moment to write down what you got from this chapter:

_____

_____

Summary

- Listen to the message; ignore the vehicle.
- The feelings you experience as you imagine your success are crucial.
- Revel in those feelings daily.
- Just as misery loves company, so does success.

Which one would you rather share? Joy of course!

Chapter 27

It's Not What You Say; It's How You Say It

Does that mean words aren't important? No, but it does mean there is more going on, especially in a face-to-face conversation, than the words you say. And you know that's true. Have you ever heard someone say, "It's not what she said, it's how she said it"? My daughter only has to say one word "Mum" and I know exactly what sort of conversation we're about to have. Why do some conversations go completely pear shaped? To counteract that conversational cringe, Dr Albert Mehrabian's Communication Model provides some clues. It's an excellent model because it provides a simple, insightful structure to help figure out why your last conversation was a disaster. This model has been mistaught in many training sessions and seminars. Presenters teach this model as applying to all types of communication. That's not true. This model is a useful tool for understanding communication that involves feelings or an attitude. We're talking an attitude of entitlement, a righteous attitude, a superior attitude, an inferior attitude to name just a few. For example, someone saying "I love your new BMW!" but saying it with a certain tone may be interpreted as "I am unimpressed at your vulgar display of wealth." Mehrabian's model cleverly shows how people can interpret your message if you use words that are not congruent with your non-verbal communication.

"I know you think you understand what you thought I said, but I'm not sure you realize that what you heard is not what I meant."
– Alan Greenspan

This quote clearly demonstrates we need all the help we can get.

The Communication Model and how it works

Workshop participants are asked the following question prior to revealing the Communication Model formula. "During an average working day, what percentage of your communication involves an attitude or an emotion?" Further examples of attitude include superiority, aloofness, entitlement, victimhood and cockiness. Examples of emotion are anger, frustration, revenge, depression, boredom and anxiety. Over 12,500 people from a wide range of industries and workplace environments pondered this question. Regardless of their working environment, the answer is always surprisingly standard. Before I reveal that percentage, how would you answer based on your current environment? How do you think your family would answer this question?

Believe it or not, 97 per cent of all answers state between 80-100 per cent. Think about that for a moment. Even if 80-100 per cent of their daily communication doesn't involve conversations that revolve around feelings or an attitude, they think it does. How much do you think that perception contributes to their levels of stress?

Let's say that figure is only 50 per cent. In that case, Prof. Albert Mehrabian's Communication Model is still well worth taking note of.

Why this is important

Have *you* ever had a conversation go terribly wrong and not understood why? Rehashing that same conversation with a friend, you confidently use the same words and ask for feedback. "I didn't say anything wrong!" you protest. And that's why this model is so important. Your friend only gets an insight into part of the conversation. The words. (Even then, are you now using the same words?) But words are only part of the scenario. Your friend has no clue about the tone of voice you used. She also didn't see the real message conveyed by your non-verbal communication (body language). This model gives you an understanding of the total message received by the other person in a face-to-face conversation.

During a face-to-face conversation, your message is delivered in three ways: words, tone and body language. Most people have little clue what their tone of voice and body language are saying. That's where the Communication Model is invaluable. It helps you understand the importance of each component. Indeed, it helps clarify the three ways you deliver face-to-face communication.

Please note the following percentages are only meant to show the relative values of each type of communication i.e. How big the slice of the pie is in terms of words versus tone and so on. In your environment, the pie may be slightly bigger or smaller. Use this model as a benchmark to compare with your situational pie.

If words are only part of the meaning of the message, and they are, what percentage would you give them?

WORDS: Seven per cent of the meaning of the message

Only seven per cent? Many express disbelief at this percentage and ask if that means words don't count. Seven per cent actually shows how important words are and how we miss the opportunity to use words in a way that influences conversations. The use of rubbish words, or threatening words, or swearing instead of choosing words that will work to communicate effectively further diminish the effectiveness of the seven per cent rule.

Solution: If the current conversation is sliding into a critical state, stop! Yes, just stop talking and breath. This sounds easy, it isn't. You'll need to practise this. Taking this pause is the perfect strategy for right now. You need time to assess what's really going on, and so does the other person. Take the pause. When you do start talking again, be concise with your words. Use a lower tone and talk slightly slower. Want to get your point across more effectively? A renowned voice coach advises to speak slower and lower.

Speak Slower and Lower

"*Words. So powerful. They can crush a heart, or heal it. They can shame a soul, or liberate it. They can shatter dreams, or energise them. They can obstruct connection, or invite it. They can create defences, or melt them. We have to use words wisely.*" – Jeff Brown

As soon as we hear a superior tone, or put-down tone, or intimidating tone or whining tone, we stop listening. "Don't talk to me like that!" you angrily respond. Is it really the words you're responding to? Take note of this next time.

Have you ever been puzzled at the offence someone has taken to something you said? Totally perplexed, did you ask yourself "What was it I said?" Like many, you do not consider the tone of voice used. Instead, the listener is labelled as sensitive or grumpy or difficult to get along with. There are no lack of labels used to make sense of a situation we don't understand.

The scary thing is most of us have no clue about the tone of voice we use. In challenging conversations, do you revert to the tone of voice your mother or your father used?

When women get emotional, their voices tend to rise to a high, sometimes shrill, pitch. Combine this high pitch with talking faster and we have a style of communicating some people find difficult to listen to. You may not do this, but I'm sure you've heard women who do. This tone lacks authority. Now, I'm not suggesting you start speaking like a man. That would be silly. But do notice the difference in reaction to a slower, lower tone of voice. Women are capable of talking lower than they normally would. Why not play around with this idea? From my personal experience, using a lower tone of voice gets a different response.

Speaking with authority

As a corporal in the Australian Army Reserve, it was fascinating to see how other corporals commanded their squads. Many shouted and swore to get their point across. All those military reality TV shows are true. However, I never had to resort to shouting. When I raised the volume of my voice and spoke in a low and slow tone, my squad knew they were in trouble. Worked every time.

Many women do not realise or use the power of their voice. Our voice is a magical instrument that can entertain, explain and persuade. If you're inclined to always talk in a monotone, even levelled sort of way, then stop doing that. Be playful with your tone. You will be a much more interesting talker and have much more power. Don't be boring.

<u>BODY LANGUAGE: 55 per cent of the meaning of the message</u>

As you can see, this is the biggie. Again, so many are not aware of the language of their body. This is really non-verbal communication, but most people know it as body language, so I'll continue to refer to it as that. Have you ever looked at the body language in photos and wondered "Whoa! What's going on there?" I remember seeing a Facebook photo of a married friend on holiday in Thailand. She was sitting with a group of friends, but her body language made it very clear one of the friends was a 'friend with benefits'. It took a while, but eventually her husband no longer featured in her cover photo.

Watch those folded arms

Let's look at what it means when we fold our arms. I can already hear you protesting "But it's comfortable" or "I'm feeling cold." Sure, they are valid reasons why your arms are folded. But the reality is, regardless of why your arms are folded, it's how others perceive that body language. Besides, if you're having a significant conversation you cannot possibly be cold or comfortable.

When you see someone with arms folded, what does that instantly communicate to you? Here are the most common answers: they're defensive, arrogant, angry insolent, not listening and defiant.

You may not agree with any of these, but again, it's not what *you* think or perceive, or even why you are doing this; it's how the other person perceives you. And the problem is, many decide your state of mind or the position you've taken from just that one element of body language. Good communicators know to look for further clues before jumping to conclusions.

Here's another reason why you need to notice when you're folding your arms. Actually, let's do this little experiment now. First, fold your arms. Next, take a deep, deep breath and then let your breath out. Good! Now unfold your arms and take in that deep, deep breath – and let that breath out. What was different? I've done this in front of hundreds of groups and it's pretty obvious they get what the difference is. When your arms are folded, you cannot take in the amount of air needed to properly oxygenate your body. If you're having a significant conversation, you need to have that good supply of oxygen for your brain to work at its best. So, unfold your arms and breathe deeply.

How's your eye contact?

Eye contact is a great help when trying to mind read someone's real intentions. It seems more and more people are uncomfortable with eye contact. How about you? People think those who do not make eye contact must be lying. Therefore, people must be telling the truth if they look you in the eye. The truth is, those who are experienced liars know this and are very good at maintaining a steady gaze.

People who don't make eye contact are often described as shifty, bored, not listening or not wanting to acknowledge your presence.

Have you ever walked down the street and made eye contact with another person and been unable to tear your gaze away? It's like a magnetic pull and you're locked in. I've walked through a checkout counter and the person serving me did not look up, not once. Making eye contact is a basic customer service rule. If you work at a busy (aren't they all?) reception, simply making eye contact with the person waiting makes a huge difference to their level of comfort and feelings of acknowledgement. No one likes to be ignored. Of course, a smile adds immense value, yet often that's not done either.

Learning to listen

An effective and fun activity conducted during our communication workshops highlights how people react when not listened to. This activity hinges on the value of eye contact and body language as communication tools. Participants are paired up with a buddy and take turns to speak about a topic that is dear to their heart. It could be their grandchildren, last holiday, favourite TV show, photography or whatever they're passionate about.

To start, the speaker faces their buddy (the listener) and talks for three minutes about their chosen topic. The rules are the speaker cannot stop talking, no matter what their buddy does, for the entire three minutes. Their buddy must listen actively, giving full and constant eye contact to the speaker for 30 seconds. For the next 30 seconds the listener can break eye contact every now and again, but not for a long period of time. This phase is more like a natural eye contact episode where we look at someone, look away and then look back again. The final phase of the activity begins 60 seconds in and the listener has to break body contact as well. They can turn their backs, grab their phone and start texting, wave to the person behind the talker, and so on. A debrief showcases each speaker's experience, then speaker and listener swap and the activity begins again.

After conducting this listening activity with hundreds of groups, I've noticed a fascinating and common thread. It doesn't matter what industry, gender, age group or leadership level, the same issues always come up. What do you think they are?

Bear in mind both parties hear the activity directions, so everyone knows what's going to happen over the next three minutes.

Listening well is a powerful tool

Even though participants know exactly what's going to happen, the majority report losing their train of thought. Although the topic is dear to their heart, when the listener breaks eye contact, the speaker loses continuity of thought. When the listener breaks body contact, very few speakers are able to effectively continue talking.

Whilst conducting this activity with a leadership group, the CEO's feedback was revealing. He was shocked to find he couldn't maintain his line of thought. He was shocked because, being a fast thinker and talker, he often stopped listening to his direct reports because he knew what they would say next. This activity showed him how his direct reports would know he'd stop listening and how that interfered with their clarity of thought. In his role as CEO, he'd never experienced people not listening (ahem ... home might've been a different matter).

Participants were encouraged to report how they felt when eye contact then body contact was broken. Even though everyone knew this was a role play and what the rules of conduct were, it didn't stop their natural reactions. Most said they felt foolish but honestly owned up to becoming upset, even very angry, when ignored. One woman reported wanting to slap the listener when he stopped listening. Interesting huh?

Do you have the look?

The final body language element we'll discuss is 'The Look'.

What does your face reveal? Lots, according to the ancient art of face reading. Have you ever been told you have a look? The message our face imparts is the most powerful of all. Let's revisit this question. When a happy face meets a grumpy face which face wins? As discussed, most answer the happy face wins. Yet it's the grumpy face that wins. How would you describe your habitual facial expression?

Do you curl your lip? Most people pick up this unconscious gesture of disdain. Our faces betray our true feelings. Some people think they can fool the observer by maintaining a neutral expression. Those practised in the art of face reading pick up subtle signs others cannot see. Whether we're squinting our eyes, clenching our jaw or pursing our lips a keen observer notices these subtle clues to what our true feelings and thoughts might be. NLP practitioners are trained to notice the fullness of the top lip and subtle colour changes of the facial skin.

If you're keen to know about micro-expressions and what they reveal, check out Paul Ekman's website www.paulekman.com to view videos of famous and infamous celebrities, politicians and other interesting people.

Can you remember as a kid giving out the grumpy face and your mother said, "Be careful, the wind will change and your face will stay like that." Mother was right! When we habitually pull faces that create furrowed brows and etched lines, that is how our face will stay.

Coming in at 55 per cent, body language is the biggest factor in communicating the meaning of your message. Become aware of your body language.

The video has to match the audio

Have you ever bought a DVD only to find the sound did not match the visual? How frustrating was that? That's exactly what it's like when your words don't match what your body language says. The mixed messages you're sending can only cause confusion. Ultimately, what you do speaks so loudly – they cannot hear a word you say. The old school saying says it best. 'Actions speak louder than words.' And that supports why body language is 55 per cent. Your message must be congruent across all forms of communication – words, tone and body language. If your message is not congruent, your words don't matter. It's not just in the political arena people have stopped listening to what leaders say. It's what we *do* that matters most.

Awareness is the key. People may not always tell you how they feel about you, but they will always show you. Pay attention. You cannot change what you're not aware of.

<u>WILL</u> Chapter 27:
It's Not What You Say; It's How You Say It –
Three Rays of Light

1. Dr Albert Mehrabian's model illustrates how the communication pie is sliced up. Words get the smallest slice. Even if you don't agree with these percentages, take note of the outcome of non-congruent communication.
2. The major issue with communication is people don't listen. Not listening is the biggest time waster of all. The remedy is: Listen. Really listen.
3. Face reading is an insightful art. Mastery increases your ability to influence. It's worth investigating courses available in your area or available on-line.

Identify Your Ray of Light: take a moment to write down what you got from this chapter:

Summary

- What tone do you use when speaking? Most of us are unaware of it.
- Use the Communication Model to assess how your conversations are going and alter the emphasis, if appropriate.
- Speak slower and lower.
- Learn to speak with authority.
- Your body language communicates the most information.
- Things like folded arms and eye contact are important.
- Learn how to listen well, it will endear you to many.
- What does your 'look' say about you?
- The video has to match the audio.

Chapter 28
My Favourite Formula For Giving Feedback

How do you tell someone his or her behaviour is not appropriate? We expect others, especially family, to act appropriately. When these expectations are not met, we become the injured party. Due to our hurt feelings, we may resort to speaking cruel words. Enveloped in the emotion of hurt, we don't understand the impact of those words on others. Salt is rubbed into the wound when it's the other person who acts mortally offended. What a nerve, we think; I am the one who has suffered wrongdoing.

Esther Hicks on well-being

"*I have not yet decided how long I'm going to use you as my excuse to not let my well-being in. If the whole world were given an opportunity to evaluate this situation, I'm certain they would all agree with me that you are wrong. I'm so mad at you, I'm willing to give up life itself to focus on this injustice you've offered me.*"

I'm confident we all know someone who focuses solely on the many injustices they've suffered in life. I've wasted many years doing exactly this. Then one day, I finally saw that my life sucked.

I was vacuuming at the time. The relentless back and forth, back and forth of the vacuum cleaner closely resembled my thought patterns. One minute a particular injustice would flash through my mind, then I'd feel more deeply hurt, then I'd think of another sad miscarriage of justice and then I'd get angry at myself for being such a fool. You get the picture; it was not a pretty one. Finally, I decided this was not how to live life. I had to do something different! We all have this ability. All it takes is deciding we've had enough and we want something better.

We get feedback all the time. It comes in many guises. Sometimes it's a look from a friend, sometimes it's how we feel and sometimes it's simply connecting the dots. When something isn't working, notice the feedback. There is no such thing as failure, only feedback. Notice what happened, adjust, then take the next step towards what you want.

"Failure is a stepping stone to greatness." – Oprah Winfrey

Our reluctance to give feedback

Feedback forms an essential part of any leader's role. Employees need to know if there are issues with their performance. In leadership surveys conducted over six years, 8,000 participants were asked why they were reluctant to give feedback. Surprisingly, the fear of employee resentment consistently rated in the top three reasons.

And this same reason can be given for our reluctance to give feedback to family and friends when their behaviour hurts us. Because so many view giving feedback as confrontational, we often don't do it well. Due to our discomfort, we may use an inappropriate tone, waffle or use the wrong words. There are a great many self-defeating behaviours at our disposal. Sadly, the outcome often means both parties act wounded and resentful.

The following feedback formula gives you a skeleton script to hang your situational words on. All you need do is remember the three parts and the scripted words used to start each part. This tool offers you a simple way to give any person effective feedback.

The 'I' Statement

The 'I' Statement rates as my favourite feedback formula. It doesn't apply to all situations, but certainly addresses many. First, let's look at the three parts that comprise this formula: The action (or behaviour) you don't like, the impact of that behaviour on you (personally) and your preferred outcome, how you'd like them to behave from now on.

When you're angry you can't think straight. That's why you end up putting your foot in your mouth. The beauty of the 'I' Statement is each part kicks off with scripted words. All you do is hang your specific situation onto these words. You'll still need to practise. But that's all it'll take to get your head around how to deliver your feedback using this model. Here are the scripted words:

ACTION
When ...

IMPACT
I feel ... (because)

PREFERRED OUTCOME
And what I would like ...

Feedback using the 'I' Statement

<u>When</u> I'm shouted at (ACTION), <u>I feel</u> humiliated (IMPACT) <u>and what I would like</u> is that we can discuss issues and my opinion will be listened to (PREFERRED OUTCOME).

Notice the PREFERRED OUTCOME does not ask to NOT be shouted at. In this part of the formula, describe the action you want, in a positive way. The listener infers from the ACTION part you don't want to be shouted at again.

(Because) is in brackets because it's optional. In the above example, I could've said "<u>I feel</u> humiliated <u>because</u> you did this in front of my friends."

It is *essential* to use a neutral/non-defensive tone when delivering this feedback.

Noisy Neighbour

Sarah, a delightful young woman, once lived in the flat below mine. One Sunday night, she had some girlfriends over and they all sat happily on Sarah's balcony smoking, drinking and talking ... very loudly. They partied on for many hours. Clearly, it was not their lot to get up for work next morning. However, it was my lot to get up at 5am. Lying in bed listening to their raucous laughter growing louder with every round of drinks, intimate details of their lives were discussed. I felt myself getting angrier and angrier. Finally at 2am, I leapt out of bed and marched to my balcony. Then I delivered my best ever 'I' Statement: "Sarah, it's 2am. When I am kept awake by loud talking, I feel angry because I have to get up at 5am to go to work and what I would like is for you to show consideration and take your conversation inside." In the stunned silence that followed, I could hear my heart pounding loudly. Sarah apologised and they all moved inside. I do own up to not keeping the tone of my voice neutral and non-defensive.

You're hearing about this because the 'I' Statement works. It enables you to deliver clear feedback in a structured way so you have less chance of missing important parts. It's no good saying later, I wish I'd said this or said that. The 'I' Statement gives you the opportunity to formulate exactly what you need to say.

Another 'I' Statement example

Have you ever asked someone to do something for you and not been happy with their response? (Perhaps I should ask have you ever been happy with their response.) Picture yourself asking someone to help you out with a task. Did they say yes, but at the same time shrugged their shoulders, sighed and rolled their eyes? Normally, you'd do a mind read on why they did that and probably get irritated. And they'd pick that up in your tone of voice. Now you're the one who's the bad guy!

Here's where the 'I' Statement comes to the rescue because it lets the other person know your experience of the interaction. And you can determine to talk calmly. Here's how you might handle their response:

"Sally, when I asked for your help to meet my deadline I heard you say yes. I'm confused because at the same time I heard you sigh and saw you shrug your shoulders and roll your eyes. What I would like is for you to help me understand why you did that?"

Remember, tone is all!

It's so important for you to be aware of your tone of voice when saying this. If your tone is one of irritation, hurt or anger you will trip their survival strategy causing a defensive response. That often results in an escalation. Now the only thing that's guaranteed is the deadline will not be met.

When you come from a place of curiosity, you will have a better chance of naturally using an appropriate tone. In turn, this increases the likelihood of a useful response. If you decide to ask Sally why she responded the way she did, you may find Sally is genuinely unaware of her behaviour. Further supporting the fact many are unaware of their habitual behaviour, yes even you.

If you rely on your mind read of what Sally's response means, you may inadvertently be the cause of ensuing conflict. Looking at a work environment, let's say Sally is a member of your team. She's a good worker. Many supervisors rely on their good workers to get the job done. They don't realise they overload good workers with more than their fair share. This happens a lot in the workplace. So Sally goes into overwhelm because it looks like she'll have to work through her lunch break today, again. You see her automatic response to your request and think she's just being difficult. Sally will likely have no clue how she responded.

Incidentally, I share Sally's 'I' Statement example in many of my workshops. Participants are asked if they could use these words. An enthusiastic nodding of heads shows this formula is appreciated. However, as one would expect, not all warm to this way of providing feedback. One woman reacted angrily and said she would never use it because she felt it was quite aggressive. This has been the most extreme negative response so far. Some have said they wouldn't feel confident to use it (What would Sally think?). Many more have been pleased to finally have a way to address what turns out to be a common situation. And it would appear to be a common situation both at home and in the workplace. Very occasionally, someone will mention it sounds condescending. If you have a habit of talking in a condescending way, everything you say will sound condescending. Remember the Communication Model? The tone of your voice is a clear indicator of your true thoughts and feelings. Coming from a true place of curiosity is the answer.

Children love the 'I' Statement. It's clear and simple and lays out all the important parts of the feedback in an easily digestible way. Why not get used to using it? It's a valuable tool in your wise woman's arsenal.

Practise, practise and practise

If you choose to work with this feedback model, please practise. One way to do this is to reflect on your day and notice where you could've used it. Then write out your 'I' Statement using that given situation. Next, read out your written 'I' Statement three times. Do this for at least five days, until you're comfortable with saying those scripted words. Getting comfortable with the format and flow of the 'I' Statement will help you speak your truth. I guarantee you could use this formula every day and few will even notice. Own it, make it yours and it will work to help you provide true feedback that is well received.

Additionally, laying out the situation on paper gives you a clearer picture of what's really going on. So remember to write out your 'I' Statements. This is a valuable habit. The 'I' Statement is another tool in your confidence kit, but it will be a useless tool if you don't use it every day.

The Reverse 'I' Statement

The Reverse 'I' Statement is an effective tool to use on yourself.

How to use this method. Consider a situation where you felt uncomfortable and wanted to work out why you felt that way. The Reverse 'I' Statement is excellent for gaining that clarity.

Situation: <u>When</u> I walk into upmarket boutiques, <u>I feel</u> inferior <u>because</u> ... <u>and what I would like</u> is to walk in confidently, just like I do when walking into my local supermarket.

The value here is working out what the 'because' part is. Even if diving deeper doesn't reveal why one feels inferior, apart from the sometimes superior attitude of the sales person, it can still be useful to write your story out in this format. For one thing, it may help illustrate how ridiculous it is to hold this story in one's head.

Here's another example: <u>When</u> I eat a whole packet of chocolate biscuits, <u>I feel</u> sick, both emotionally and physically <u>because</u> eating a whole packet causes my body to reject the toxic overload and I get disgusted with myself for that self-abuse. <u>What I would like</u> is to develop a strategy to stop my chocolate biscuit binges.

We have strategies for everything we do. When we're disciplined enough to exercise, we have a strategy for making sure we do exercise. We all have buying strategies. Those familiar with NLP know of the techniques that help identify and change habitual behaviour. If you can't stop yourself buying another pair of shoes there is an NLP strategy to help you do that. Perhaps you want to stop drinking every night of the week? There are many strategies to help 'short circuit' unwelcome behaviours. First though, you need to decide if they are unwelcome behaviours. The exact moment you truly decide a behaviour does not benefit you, in any way, you will stop doing it.

Giving and getting feedback is a necessary part of living a better life of vitality and fulfilment. Be open to feedback given by others; they might just be right.

<u>WILL</u> Chapter 28:
My Favourite Formula For Giving Feedback –
Three Rays of Light

1. Please practise the 'I' Statement every day for the next five days.
2. When you familiarise yourself with the scripted words, you will instantly respond to any situation with confidence and flair.
3. Think of a situation where you've delayed giving feedback for inappropriate behaviour. Right now, write out your 'I' Statement for that situation.

Identify Your Ray of Light: take a moment to write down what you got from this chapter:

_____

_____

Summary

- When something isn't working, notice the feedback.
- Use the 'I' statement (Action, Impact, Outcome) formula for giving feedback.
- Ensure your tone doesn't kick the other person into survival mode.
- Come from a place of curiosity.

Chapter 29
Women Don't Ask And Why You Should Ask

Do you ask for what you want? If you said yes, are you absolutely sure you do?

Last year I was asked to present workshops on negotiation skills
training. Although negotiation skills form part of our Leadership
courses, these workshops needed a slightly different perspective so
further research was needed. Surfing the net looking for new ideas
and fascinating facts is one of my favourite pastimes. Many hours
are spent curiously skipping from one page to the next. That's how
I discovered an eye-opening book written by Linda Babcock and
Sara Laschever called *Women Don't Ask*. According to the authors,
"Women don't ask for raises and promotions and better job opportunities. They don't ask for recognition for the good work they do.
They don't ask for more help at home." This book explores the personal and societal reasons women seldom ask for what they want,
need and *deserve* at home and at work.

A standard interview question was, "Are you usually successful in getting what you want?" To Babcock and Laschever's initial
surprise, almost every woman they spoke to said yes. Upon further
probing, they discovered many women felt they were successful at
getting what they wanted, in part, because they didn't want very
much.

The skill of asking in negotiations

I'm sure you won't be surprised to find out women do indeed
behave differently to men when they negotiate. Men are inclined

'to take no prisoners' to win at all costs. Women are inclined to negotiate in a collaborative way.

There are other differences:

- In surveys, two and a half times more women than men said they feel a great deal of apprehension about negotiation.
- Men initiate negotiations about four times as often as women.
- Women are more pessimistic about how much is available and so they typically ask for, and get, less.
- Women often worry more than men about the impact their actions will have on the relationship.
- Fear that people around them will react badly if they ask for too much.

According to Babcock and Laschever, by neglecting to negotiate her starting salary, a woman may sacrifice over half a million dollars in earnings by the end of her career. You may wish to reread that ... over half a million dollars.

An inconvenient truth

Before turning the first page of *Women Don't Ask,* my response to whether or not I asked was a resounding "Of course I do!" Turning the pages of each chapter, it became painfully clear I was not good at asking. Since reading this book, I've asked! This has resulted in upgrades to grander rooms in hotels, negotiating cheaper rates for hire cars and working out better deals in training contracts. Looking someone in the eye and asking if that's their best price is not a problem anymore. I deserve the best deal and so do you. So ask for it!

Another truth is women expect significant others to know what they want and need. The dilemma is how these others discover these wants and needs. Magic must be involved because words are rarely involved. Women expect the other to know! To ensure never falling into this trap, I don't expect others to possess mind reading skills. Details are communicated clearly (even if I think they 'should' know).

WILL Chapter 29:
Women Don't Ask And Why You Should Ask –
Three Rays of Light

1. Grab *Women Don't Ask*. It's available on Amazon and is well worth your time.
2. This book highlights a situation involving a male and female manager. Both were considered for promotion. But as the woman achieved much better results than the man, it seemed a given she would get the promotion. You've guessed she didn't. When she angrily confronted her boss, his response was he didn't know she wanted the promotion. The male manager had asked, so he got it. I know ...
3. Looking at your situation in life, what are you not asking for?

Identify Your Ray of Light: take a moment to write down what you got from this chapter:

_____

_____

Summary

- Learn to ask for what you want.
- People can't read minds – so ask!

Chapter 30

This Is Your Life:
WILL TAKE ACTION

What will you do to make the rest of your life the best of your life?

Looking back on Part Four, and considering all those events and elements conspiring to shape your life so far, this chapter has to be written by you.

Please take the time to jot down your thoughts and feelings after reading this part.

Consider the following as you write. Do you know what it feels like to be the rabbit in the middle of the road? Do you feel you're too old to create your RoadMAP? Are you able to control your feelings? How does the Communication Model impact on the results you're getting in your life? Will you practise and use the 'I' Statement? Do you ask, and if you do, do you get what you ask for? Do you ask for enough?

Part Four is a wake-up call, revealing strategies to support you in creating a better life. But nothing changes if you don't change; if you don't take action. Remember, no one else gets to see your words. This is your life ... so write:

_____

_____

_____

_____

_____

_____

_____

Please do not continue onto PART FIVE until you've emptied your mind onto this page. It doesn't need to make sense, just do it! You may need to use extra sheets of paper. Keep writing until there is nothing more to write.

Finally, this space is for identifying just one thought from all you've written in Chapter 31. As you read through your own words, what is the most important, most compelling, most revealing thing you've written that jumps out and surprises or shocks you? It may be an uncomfortable truth, delight in that for designing a new life begins with awareness of the old.

"Out with the old, in with the True." – Jeff Brown

_____

_____

_____

_____

Go where you're celebrated.
Not where you're tolerated.

www.Over60StillFabulous.com

PART FIVE:
WOW A CELEBRATION

We've made it to the last part. WOW! A celebration of you and your life's journey. WOW is about embracing fun. WOW acknowledges a joyful, meaningful existence is within everyone's reach, if we would but reach for it. WOW says "I did it!"

After a long life of habitual behaviour and ingrained responses, can women over 60 leap the Chasm of Loss: loss of our youth, loss of our freedom, loss of love, loss of our health, our mobility, our vibrancy and our very identity? Can we relocate from the 'Island of Lack' to the 'Island of More'? Can we truly believe we have a gift, that our life has significance, that we make a difference to this world? Yes, yes and yes!

WOW also stands for Women of Wisdom. *You* are a Woman of Wisdom. Embrace your power; stand for what you believe. Be courageous, be confident, be you.

> ## If *we* do not believe this, no one will.

PART FIVE asks what made the glass so empty and looks at our choice of empowering words. Time to do a stocktake. Are your values still the same as determined at the beginning of this book? Next, a revealing look at the years remaining and an important question. And finally we consider what the real meaning of life is.

Chapter 31

Words Of Wisdom From The Masculine

I hope you found words in my book that captured your heart and inspired you to see the light illuminating the dark. When I came across this excerpt from Jeff Brown's book *Love It Forward*, his words captured my heart:

"DRINKING FROM AN EMPTY GLASS - A NOTE TO A DEAR DARK FRIEND

Yes, I know the government is corrupt. Yes, I know there are people conspiring. Yes, I know people can lack integrity. Yes, I know that western culture is materialistic. Yes, I know that corporations are self-serving. Yes, I know that the media is manipulative. I share many of your concerns.

And I also know that we cannot change the world without acknowledging what is wrong. I know that we must stand against that which shames, oppresses and damages humanity. I know that we should not ignore the injustices and put on a fake smile. I know that we must find our voice and stand our ground. I know that we must fight for our right to the light. I believe deeply in forward moving criticism.

But something doesn't feel quite right. You complain all the time. You have made negativity a full-time job. You don't make an effort to find solutions. You blame everything on the world out there. You don't actually do anything positive to effect change.

And you seldom acknowledge the positive steps humanity has made. You seldom acknowledge the beauty around you. You almost never see the light in the darkness. I know something from my lived experience. I know that the light is always there. It is there, in the breath that keeps you alive, in the smile of a child, in the one more chance to find your path.

It is there in the rise of the feminine, in the therapeutic revolution, in the burgeoning quest for authenticity. If you can't see it, then the issue is a personal one, for there are signs of progress everywhere.

And I also know from a lifetime of overcoming that it is possible to hold it all at once. To fight against injustice while still embodying the light. To see where we are lacking, while rejoicing in our abundance. To express our anger, and to live our gratitude. To feel overwhelmed by an unfair world, while still achieving our goals. To admit how far we have yet to travel, while applauding how far we have come.

And so I wonder what lives below your perpetual negativity? Apart from the problems with the world, what happened that darkened your lens? What made the glass so empty? Is it really all about the world 'out there', or are there also unresolved personal experiences that need to be healed?

What are you really trying to express about the lack of love, attention, and satisfaction in your life? What is your deeper complaint? What lives below this victimhood? What needs to be expressed and resolved so that you will see some light shining through again? Please don't wait until the world is perfect, for it will never be so. Dear friend, how can I help you to believe again?"

Reprinted with permission

This passage, from Jeff Brown's book, delivers some powerful messages and deserves to be read more than once.

Words are powerful, especially the written word. When reading the written word, we cannot be misled by our interpretation of another's tone of voice and body language. Words sit silently on the page, challenging us to make sense of their meaning. The gift of the wordsmith involves playing with the placement, choice and tempo of words in such a way to influence and persuade the reader, without their conscious knowledge. Even so, interpretation of the meaning of the message rests squarely on our shoulders.

Powerful words

Abundance. This powerful word vibrates through me and feels good. There are many uplifting letter formations: compassion, harmony, joy, embrace, flower, blossom, nature, flourish, brilliant, happiness, laughter, cherish, kindness, magic, light, stardust, Gaia, love, beauty, affection, peace, sacred, power and enrich. Do you have a favourite?

Dr Masaru Emoto's experiments demonstrated the incredible effect of words on water. Remember our bodies are up to 75 per cent water. We must choose

> **The words you speak become the house you live in.**

our words carefully. The words you use determine where you live, and that doesn't mean what you think it does.

Living on the 'Island of More'

We already know living on the 'Island of More' does not mean the possession of more stuff. You can possess more stuff, more shoes, more diamonds, more houses and more cars, yet still live on the 'Island of Lack'. Am I contradicting my earlier words about being rich and happy? No, you absolutely can be rich and happy. The secret is simple. To be both rich and happy you need to know what you truly value, above and beyond anything else. Only then can you truly appreciate what you have. Regardless of what people say, money does not sit at the top of the tree. That's where the faerie sits and we all know faeries aren't real, don't we? But I digress.

"The real voyage of discovery consists not in seeking new landscapes but in having new eyes." – Marcel Proust

Living on the 'Island of More' means you live life with deep appreciation for that which you value. Think about this, if you do not appreciate what you already have, it is not possible for you to appreciate more. To truly appreciate, you must practise gratitude. To do that, you must know those things you deeply value in life. At the start of this book, you determined your top three values in life.

After reading through the chapters, are your values still the same? It will be a worthwhile exercise to flush out your values again. You may well be surprised.

<u>WOW</u> Chapter 31:
Words Of Wisdom From The Masculine –
Three Rays of Light

1. In an excerpt from his book *Love It Forward*, Jeff Brown writes about drinking from an empty glass and seeing the light in the darkness. What value did you glean from this excerpt?
2. List five of your powerful feel-good words.
3. What are the top three values you hold for your life?

Identify Your Ray of Light: take a moment to write down what you got from this chapter:

_____

_____

Summary

- Jeff Brown asks you to examine what made the glass so empty.
- Don't let your interpretations colour another's words.
- To be rich and happy you need to know what you truly value.
- Practise gratitude.

Chapter 32
Life Is Short; Buy The Shoes

"I still have my feet on the ground, I just wear better shoes." – Oprah Winfrey

Surely we all want our lives to be a meaningful and enjoyable experience? As stated throughout this book, this relies solely on your interpretation of everyday events. Not wanting to own this part of their life's journey, many rely on external solutions, such as drugs, alcohol and TV. But these only serve to dull and distract the mind. No matter how life has been or is now, we all have the ability to take a different course.

Our beginning does not define our end.

Eleanor Roosevelt was a lonely, neurotic young girl; as a child, Thomas Edison was sickly, poor and believed to be retarded by his teachers; Albert Einstein's early years were filled with anxieties and disappointments. Yet they all ended up creating powerful and useful lives.

Our rigid rules

As we age, our own rigid rules deeply define not only our lives, but all those in our lives. Last year, an older woman shared how she refused to spend all her time with her older friends. "They're too rigid!" she said. Her preferred company included a mix of younger people. Their company helped her view life in a different way, which caused her to feel more vibrant and more alive. Her words reminded me of a quote from Jim Rohn "You are the average of the five people you spend the most time with." You may recall Jim Rohn presented at my very first personal development seminar a long, long time ago. If only I'd 'heard' the wisdom of those words then. Your current life situation reflects your beliefs and your values. Look around; if you don't like what you see ... change it. If you like the shoes, buy them!

"You're going to find a freedom beyond description when you give up trying to control the uncontrollable." – Abraham-Hicks

Your 'end of book' reality check

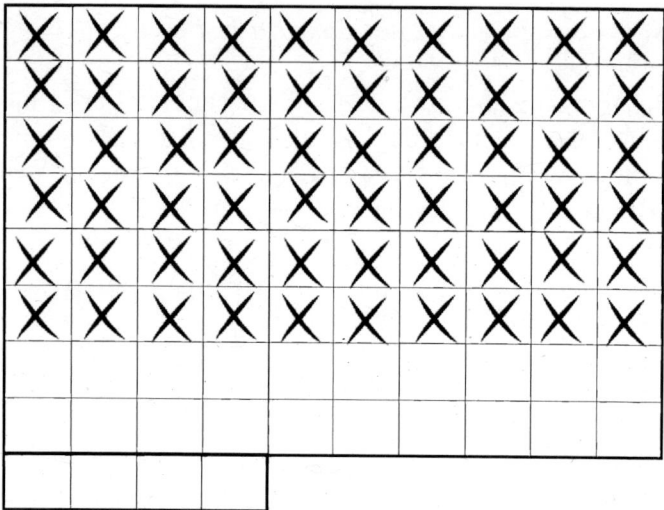

Looking at this table, notice there are 60 crosses already marked. As a woman over 60, please now complete the table by marking a cross in each vacant box for each year of your current age over 60. For example, if your age is 65, you only need mark a cross in five more boxes.

The life span for women in Western countries sits at around 85 years. This is normally a government prediction and does not doom you to that designated end of life. *You* determine your own 'end date'. You predict your years on this 'mortal plane'. Do not leave your destiny in the hands of others. However, using the government projection of around 85 years, how do you choose to live the rest of your years?

Time to revisit the top five regrets of people on their deathbeds:

1. I wish I'd had the courage to live a life true to myself, not the life others expected of me.
2. I wish I didn't work so hard.
3. I wish I'd had the courage to express my feelings.
4. I wish I'd stayed in touch with my friends.
5. I wish I'd let myself be happier.

Point five needs highlighting:
"Many did not realise, until the end, that happiness is a choice. They'd stayed stuck in old patterns and habits. Fear of change had them pretending to others, and to themselves, they were content. But deep within, they'd longed to laugh properly and have silliness in their life again."

Which of these regrets do you have right now? Which one will you cross off the list first? Own your power to enrich the years to come. There are many roads to take, why not drive down a new one? Imagine how different our world would be if we hit the delete button on fear and greed. Live your dreams. Don't just dream about living.

"Out of Your Dreams: Be Born, Out of Your Heart: Be Alive, Out of Your Soul: Be Light" – Bashar

Trees and stars

My life view compares people to trees: firmly grounded and at the same time, reaching for the stars. In recognition of this view, the five-pointed star forms part of my business logo. I also use the tree as a symbol to interpret and present many complex concepts controlling our lives. Apart from that, stars and trees form part of the intricate and beautiful fabric of our everyday life. Whilst I've never hugged a star, I sometimes feel compelled to hug a tree. It feels good.

Give yourself permission to reach for the stars. Give yourself permission to celebrate.

Give yourself permission to live this moment.

"*When the compulsive striving away from the now ceases, the joy of being flows into everything you do. The moment your attention turns to the Now, you feel a presence, a stillness, a peace.*" – Eckhart Tolle

When you experience sadness or regret, your mind has taken you into your past. When you experience anxiety or stress, your mind has taken you into your future. Notice how little time we spend in the now moment. Alan Watt's words ring true here: "No valid plans for the future can be made by those who have no capacity for living now." The many and varied quotes throughout this book have taken years to compile. Sometimes, the clever placement of words is enough to hit home. Just a few well-chosen words can cause a person to shift focus, to change habitual behaviour patterns. One small change can start the snowball effect of changing your entire life. Are you ready?

What is the meaning of life?

According to Mihaly Csikszentmihalyi, the answer is astonishingly simple. The meaning of life *is* meaning: whatever it is, wherever it comes from, it is a unified purpose that gives meaning to life. However, most of us become so rigidly fixed in the ruts carved out by genetic programming and social conditioning, we ignore the options of choosing any other course of action. You choose the game. You play the cards. You decide which road to travel. It's your interpretation of your life that gives it meaning.

We've already looked at the powerful effect two little words can have on the meaning of your life. Please now reflect on these two ancient words and the wisdom contained within: "Know Thyself."

<u>WOW</u> Chapter 32:
Life Is Short; Buy The Shoes – Three Rays of Light

1. "You are the average of the five people you spend the most time with." Take time to think this through. Notice the effect on your life.
2. After marking the crosses to match your current age, how did you feel?
3. What is your favourite quote?

Identify Your Ray of Light: take a moment to write down what you got from this chapter:

_____

_____

Summary

- Our beginning does not define our end.
- Consider Jim Rohn's words 'You are the average of the five people you spend the most time with'.
- Happiness is a choice.
- Reach for the stars, celebrate, stay in the moment.

Chapter 33
This Is Your Life:
WOW A CELEBRATION

What will you do to make the rest of your life the best of your life? Looking back on Part Five, and considering all those events and elements conspiring to shape your life so far, this chapter has to be written by you.

Please take the time to jot down your thoughts and feelings after reading this part.

Consider the following as you write: Words of Wisdom from the masculine, powerful words, a reflushing out of your values, the meaning of life. Life is short; Buy the shoes.

Part Five is a wake-up call, revealing strategies to support you in creating a better life. But nothing changes if you don't change, if you don't take action. Remember, no one else gets to see your words. This is your life ... so write:

_____

_____

_____

_____

_____

_____

_____

_____

_____

_____

_____

_____

_____

Please empty your mind onto this page. It doesn't need to make sense, just do it! You may need to use extra sheets of paper. Keep writing until there is nothing more to write.

Finally, this space is for identifying just one thought from all you've written in Chapter 33. As you read through your own words, what is the most important, most compelling, most revealing thing you've written that jumps out and surprises or shocks you? It may be an uncomfortable truth, delight in that, for designing a new life begins with awareness of the old.

"Out with the old, in with the True." Jeff Brown

_____

_____

_____

_____

Chapter 34
Putting It All Together

This chapter pulls together all your 'Just one thought' realisations from previous chapters to display them on one page. Perhaps, as you read through them, one last logical conclusion may become very clear.

PART ONE: NOW I'M HERE – Page 72

My most important, most compelling, most revealing thought from this part is:

_____

_____

PART TWO: HOW I GOT HERE – Page 132

My most important, most compelling, most revealing thought from this part is:

_____

_____

PART THREE: WHAT I WANT – Page 158

My most important, most compelling, most revealing thought from this part is:

_____

_____

PART FOUR: WILL TAKE ACTION – *Page 204*

My most important, most compelling, most revealing thought from this part is:

_____

_____

PART FIVE: WOW A CELEBRATION – *Page 220*

My most important, most compelling, most revealing thought from this part is:

_____

_____

My Logical Conclusion

_____

_____

Chapter 35

We Are The Elders Of Our Time

Let's start acting like that.

This entire book has led to this chapter. I strongly believe women over 60 are the 'Elders of Our Time'. We are the leaders and role models for the younger generation. Traditionally, it's up to our generation to show the way, to guide and shape the lives of our young ones. It's up to us to share our wisdom, courage and confidence. And we can only do this when we step into our own power, when we speak our truth.

You may say, but who will listen? If we see injustice, suffering, pain and wrongdoing, yet choose to stay in our comfort zone then no one will listen. We will remain invisible, pampered and power-less, considered a burden on society.

"*We could never learn to be brave and patient, if there were only joy in the world.*" – Helen Keller

Am I saying you need to be an activist? No! But you could be. Am I saying use your considerable skills and talents to rise in politics? No! But you could do that if you so desired. Am I saying chain yourself to the railings around your buildings of political power (like the Suffragettes)? No! But you may choose to do that too.

Use your personal power

Connect to your own personal power, for it is immense. I am saying to stand in that power and operate from that place, for you will make a difference. Who will that difference impact? Maybe your grandchildren, and that is enough. Maybe a group of 'oldens' in your area, and that is enough. Maybe you'll shine the light into the darkness of those living on the edge of society, and that is enough. Maybe you'll become a speaker and talk to the heart of all those willing to hear, and that is enough.

Maybe you'll simply stand straighter and walk with more dignity and self-respect, and that is enough. Whatever your desire to make a difference, to leave a legacy, will be enough. Simply the decision to create instead of constant consuming is enough. FOR YOU ARE ENOUGH and what you choose to do from the heart has the power to change our planet. Our planet needs more people who care enough to step up, each in their own way.

"Understand that the right to choose your own path is a sacred privilege. Use it. Dwell in possibility." – Oprah Winfrey

Some say "Over 60 and over the hill" but they're wrong about that. We are a benefit to this world, not a burden. Don't ever doubt your worth. There's a reason you're still alive, why not find out what it is? To do that, you must step up and take accountability for your own life. If your life is dull and meaningless, do something about that. Do something different to change your life, for you are the only one who can. We are long past waiting for that knight in shining armour to whisk us away to a happy ever after.

It's time to realise we are the people we've been waiting for.

Epilogue
My Big Passionate Idea

"Never doubt that a small group of thoughtful, committed citizens can change the world; indeed, it's the only thing that ever has."
– Margaret Mead

And that small group of thoughtful, committed citizens has only ever started with one. Great movements have changed the history of our world and they've always started with that one person sharing their big passionate idea with others.

Now is the time to share my big passionate idea, my ulterior motive, with you. In line with the messages in this book, I wish to form a special group for single women over 60. This group, called 'The Inner Circle of Elders', is a courageous fledgling group who intend to make a local difference with a global impact. We wish to leave a legacy for the children of the future. Our hope is the children of earth *will have* a future. Reading this book is a first step.

If this excites you (or scares you), please email me to find out more: victoriarose@innercircleofelders.com

The Road Ahead

Thank you for reading *How To Make The Rest Of Your Life The Best Of Your Life: Tough Love For Smart Single Women Over 60.*

As you worked through each part, did you complete all the activities? The revelation of who you really are can only come with your full participation. You are worth the time and the effort it takes to stand, fully illuminated, in the light of your truth. Embrace your right to be celebrated, not just tolerated. It takes courage to step outside your comfort zone, but that's where life truly begins. If you haven't done so, please go back and complete each activity.

To travel the road ahead, to avoid taking the same old highways and byways, you must change yourself. You can do that! If you choose that.

The Fork In The Road Ahead

The fork in the road ahead signifies a choice you must make: the high road or the low road.

The low road means you're done. It's all too hard. Perhaps you like the same old highways and byways anyway. It's your choice to travel the same route every day of your life. Recognise it is your choice. Don't drive into Blame Boulevard and expect people to keep listening to the same old tirade. You will end up in Lonely Lane. I guarantee it.

The high road means you found the nuggets of gold hidden in every chapter. Already, you've made changes. It's not easy. But it's doable. And it's exciting! You may wish for some support on your journey. Here are ways to stay in touch with me:

Email: victoriarose@over60stillfabulous.com
Get our 'Women Of Wisdom' quotes: www.over60stillfabulous.com
Follow on Facebook: www.facebook.com/victoriarosetrainer
Join me on Linkedin: www.linkedin.com/victoriarosetrainer
Join me on Twitter: @honorose

Be part of a one-day event based on my five step formula: From NOW to WOW.

Develop deeper into 'you' during this interactive and fun session: www.theleadershipvoice.com

The ultimate five-day retreat in Ubud, Bali. One day is devoted to each of the five steps. Join a small group of supportive women and fully live the experience of From NOW to WOW. Be enveloped by the peace, love and delight that is Ubud.

www.over60bali.com

Enquire about my Inner Circle of Elders
victoriarose@innercircleofelders.com

The world needs women just like you.

Those women prepared to step up and claim their role as Elders of Our Time.

Can we talk?

Acknowledgements

My children are at the top of the list. They've taught me many lessons and given me many reasons to be proud to be their Mum. Thank you.

I acknowledge those many friends and acquaintances who conspired to shape my life's journey. It's been a rocky, slippery road at times, and I didn't always want to hear your words of wisdom. But here we are, still travelling together. Thank you.

Over the years, many workshop participants shared their wisdom on how to develop and grow as caring human beings. They laughed, learnt and lingered longer to share private stories. Thank you.

Finally, I thank you.

You have no idea what it means to me to know you have stepped into and embraced the reality of living a better life. Please let me know how you go.

Recommended Reading

Csikszentmihalyi M, 1991, *FLOW* HarpersCollins, New York

Ellison SS, 2009, *Taking the War Out of Our Words*, Wyatt-Mc-Kenzie Publishing

Babcock L, Laschever S, 2007, *Women Don't Ask*, Bantam Dell

Heath C, Heath D, 2007, *Made to Stick*, Random House

Griffiths A, 2007, *101 Ways to Have a Business and a Life*, Allen & Unwin, Australia

Priestley D, 2011, *Become a Key Person of Influence*, Ecademy Press, England

Luana E, 1990, *BASHAR: Blueprint For Change*

Eckhart T, 2004, The *Power of NOW*, Hodder Headline Australia Pty Ltd